Excel 2007
Pocket Guide

SECOND EDITION

Excel 2007
Pocket Guide

Curt Frye

Beijing · Cambridge · Farnham · Köln · Paris · Sebastopol · Taipei · Tokyo

Excel 2007 Pocket Guide, Second Edition
by Curt Frye

Published by O'Reilly Media, Inc., 1005 Gravenstein Highway North, Sebastopol, CA 95472.

O'Reilly books may be purchased for educational, business, or sales promotional use. Online editions are also available for most titles (*safari.oreilly.com*). For more information, contact our corporate/institutional sales department: (800) 998-9938 or *corporate@oreilly.com*.

Editor: Simon St.Laurent	**Indexer:** Ellen Troutman Zaig
Production Editor: Marlowe Shaeffer	**Cover Designer:** Karen Montgomery
Proofreader: Marlowe Shaeffer	**Interior Designer:** David Futato
	Illustrator: Jessamyn Read

Printing History:

September 2003:	First Edition.
October 2007:	Second Edition.

ISBN-10: 0-596-51452-2
ISBN-13: 978-0-596-51452-5

[TM]

Contents

CHAPTER 1

Understanding Excel

The first chapter of this book is designed to give those readers with relatively little experience using Excel 2007 enough information to dive right in and start creating rich Excel workbooks immediately, and to fill in some of the details for more experienced Excel users who haven't had enough time to examine the program and its new user interface in depth.

This chapter covers:

- What's new in Excel 2007
- The Excel interface
- Workbook, template, and workspace files
- The anatomy of an Excel file
- Formatting
- Shortcut Menus and the Mini Toolbar (a.k.a. the "floatie")

What's New in Excel 2007

After the significant leap forward from Excel 95 to Excel 97, Excel versions 2000, 2002, and 2003 were incremental improvements on the same basic application design. By contrast, Excel 2007 is a substantial departure from Excel 2003. Excel 2007 comes with a new user interface (detailed later in this chapter), a much larger worksheet, and new formatting capabilities, among many other changes. Table 1-1 summarizes the most important changes in Excel 2007.

Table 1-1. Excel 2007 greatly expands the size of the worksheet and extends the possible number of sorting levels, characters in a cell, and colors in a workbook.

Capability	Old limit	New limit
Worksheet size	65,536 rows by 256 columns	1,048,576 rows by 16,384 columns
Total characters in a cell	1,024 characters	32,767 characters
Total characters printed in a cell	1,024 characters	32,767 characters
Colors in a workbook	56	16 million colors
Undo levels	16	100
Sort levels	3	64
Conditional format conditions	3	Limited by available memory
Maximum length of a formula	1,024 characters	8,192 characters
Maximum number of arguments to a function	30	255
Number of nested levels allowed in a formula	7	64

NOTE

The new limits only apply when you save a workbook using the new Office 2007 file format. If you save a workbook using the old Excel 97–2003 file format, the old limits apply.

The Excel 2007 Interface

Excel's interface stayed more or less constant from Excel 97 to Excel 2003. During that time, the program's developers added some new features and moved items around in the menu and toolbar system, but the basic structure remained the same. All that changed in Office 2007.

The Ribbon

Excel 2007, Word 2007, and PowerPoint 2007 all use the new Microsoft Office Fluent interface design, commonly referred to as the *Ribbon* (Figure 1-1).

Office Button

Figure 1-1. The Home tab of the new Excel 2007 user interface Ribbon.

Figure 1-1 shows one tab from the new Ribbon user interface, which replaces the menu bars and toolbars (collectively known as command bars) found in Excel 2003. The Ribbon contains most, but not all, of the commands available in Excel 2007. The Microsoft Office user experience team created the new Ribbon interface in an effort to make it easier to discover the full range of built-in capabilities in Excel 2007. The Office product teams constantly receive requests for features that were already built into the programs, so they designed the new interface and applied it to the three most popular Office programs.

NOTE

The Ribbon resizes itself and its controls to reflect your monitor's resolution and the window size, so you might see a different set of controls (and differently appearing controls) than is shown in Figure 1-1.

Rather than force users to poke through a maze of menus, toolbars, and dialog boxes to find the commands they're looking for, the Ribbon brings most of Excel's functionality to the top level of the user interface. The Home tab, shown in Figure 1-1, contains the most common operations: cutting and pasting, font and cell formatting, finding and selecting cells, and so on.

The Page Layout tab of the Ribbon (Figure 1-2) hosts buttons that enable you to change the page's appearance and control printing. For example, you can change a worksheet's margins, turn gridlines on and off, select the parts of the worksheet you want to print, and add a background image.

Figure 1-2. The controls on the Page Layout tab let you determine how your page looks when it's displayed and printed.

TIP

To hide the Ribbon, press Ctrl-F1. Pressing Ctrl-F1 again brings the Ribbon back. When the Ribbon is hidden, clicking on the menu temporarily brings the Ribbon back.

Contextual Tabs

Previous versions of Excel displayed toolbars with buttons and menus you could use to change a selected object, such as an image you inserted into a worksheet. Excel 2007 doesn't use the command bar user interface, so the designers created contextual tabs (Figure 1-3), which appear on the Ribbon when you select an object with associated controls that don't appear on the basic Ribbon.

Contextual tabs appear at the right end of the Ribbon and are a different color than the regular Ribbon tabs.

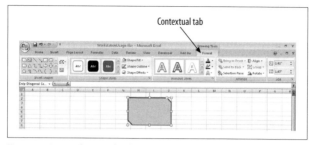

Figure 1-3. Excel 2007 displays contextual tabs when selected objects require controls that don't appear on the basic Ribbon.

Dialog Expanders

The new Excel 2007 user interface brings the most commonly used controls to the top level of the Ribbon. You'll still need to display a lot of dialog boxes to make the changes you want, particularly when it comes to page setup tasks such as changing margins. Excel 2007 indicates there's a dialog box available in two ways. First, if a Ribbon button's label is followed by three dots, clicking the button displays a dialog box. Second, some Ribbon groups have a dialog expander at the bottom-right corner of the group (see Figure 1-4). Clicking the dialog expander control displays a dialog box related to the group's controls.

Figure 1-4. When you need finer control over your worksheet, open a dialog box to display the full range of changes you can make to the selected item.

The Office Button

When using Excel 2007 for the first time, many experienced Excel users ask, "Where is the File menu?" Early drafts of the Excel 2007 interface did have a File menu at the top-left corner of the Ribbon, but the Office user interface design team removed the File menu and replaced it with the Microsoft Office Button (Figure 1-5).

Figure 1-5. You can find the familiar File menu items, such as Save, Save As, Print, and Close by clicking the Microsoft Office Button.

Quick Access Toolbar

Just to the right of the Office Button, you'll find the Quick Access Toolbar. The Quick Access Toolbar contains three buttons by default: the Save button, the Undo button (for undoing changes you just made), and the Redo/Repeat button (which lets you reverse a click of the Undo button or, depending on what you just did, repeat an operation).

You can add any Ribbon button or group to the Quick Access Toolbar by right-clicking the button or group's name and selecting the "Add to Quick Access Toolbar" menu item.

The Excel Program Window

Aside from the Ribbon, the Excel 2007 user interface has changed little from Excel 97. Figure 1-6 shows the Excel 2007 program window; the text that follows describes the elements you'll use the most.

Title bar
> The title bar, which appears at the top of the Excel window, shows the name of the workbook and any file access restrictions. If you display the Open dialog box and click the down arrow at the right edge of the Open button, you can open a selected workbook as a copy of the original in read-only mode, in repair mode, or (if the file is web-compatible) in a browser. Whichever status you select will be displayed on the title bar.

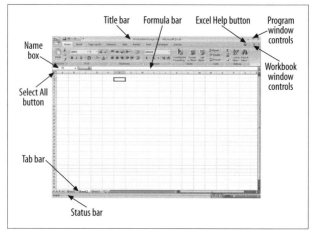

Figure 1-6. The Excel 2007 user interface.

Excel Help button

    The Excel Help button, which is a round blue button with a white question mark in the center, appears near the top-right corner of the Excel program window. Clicking the Excel Help button displays the Excel Help window, which contains links to popular topics and a search box where you can type words and phrases you'd like to look up.

Formula bar

    The formula bar displays the content of the active cell or the formula that generated that content. You edit the contents of a cell by clicking in the formula bar and using the mouse and keyboard. You can also double-click the cell and edit in it directly. (After you type the function and the opening parentheses, for example =SUM(, the program displays information about what kind of input the formula you are entering requires—e.g., the SUM formula expects one or more cell ranges.)

Name box

The name box displays the reference of the active cell (e.g., B2) or displays the size of a selected group of cells (e.g., 2R×1C, or "two rows by one column"). When the mouse button is released, a reference to the first cell selected appears in the box. The name box also lists the named ranges in the worksheet. Open the name box and select a named range to highlight the cells in that range.

TIP

You can get more information on named ranges in Chapter 2 under the section "Using Named Ranges."

Program window controls

At the top right of the Excel window are four controls: the Minimize button, which reduces the Excel program window to a button on the task bar; the Restore button, which toggles the program window between smaller and larger sizes; the Maximize button, which appears when the program window is reduced in size; and the Close button, which exits Excel.

Workbook window controls

Just below the program window controls are a similar set of controls for each open workbook. Click a workbook's Minimize button and it becomes a title bar within the larger Excel window; click the Restore button to toggle the workbook between smaller and larger sizes; click the Maximize button to expand the workbook to fill the window; and click Close to close the workbook.

Select All button

Clicking the Select All button, located at the top-left corner of a worksheet (to the left of the Column A header and above the Row 1 header), selects every cell in a worksheet. Pressing Ctrl-A does the same thing.

Tab bar

Every worksheet in a workbook is represented (at the bottom of the window) by a tab. Clicking a tab displays the corresponding worksheet, while right-clicking a tab displays a shortcut menu with options to insert a new worksheet; rename, delete, or move the selected worksheet; select all the worksheets; or access VBA code for that sheet. You can change a worksheet tab's color if you want to make it stand out from the other worksheets.

Status bar

The Excel status bar (Figure 1-7) displays the current state of the program; lists any background tasks that are running, such as saves; and displays a running summary of numerical values in currently selected cells. You can change the summary operations or turn them off.

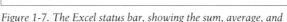

Figure 1-7. The Excel status bar, showing the sum, average, and count of selected cells in the worksheet.

New Excel 2007 File Format

One of the most significant changes between Office 2003 and Office 2007 is that the three most popular programs (Word, Excel, and PowerPoint) use a new file format that is substantially different from the format used in Excel 97–2003. The new file format, which is based on the Extensible Markup Language (XML), separates Excel 2007 workbooks into different components—creating text files where possible—and uses the ZIP compression algorithm to reduce the file's size.

Separating a workbook's worksheets, charts, drawings, printer settings, and tables into different files reduces the likelihood that a hard disk failure will ruin an entire Excel 2007 workbook. If Excel can't open part of the file, it displays an error message but opens as much of the workbook as it can.

Even though Excel 97–2003 can't open Excel 2007 files without downloading and installing additional software, Excel 2007 can open earlier files with no difficulty. When you open an Excel 97–2003 file in Excel 2007, the program opens it in Compatibility Mode, which prevents you from adding new formats, charts, drawings, or other features not present in Excel 2003. If you want to save an Excel 97–2003 file as an Excel 2007 file, which enables the new features, click Office Button → Save As and set the file type to Excel Workbook.

Workbook, Template, and Workspace Files

Excel 2007 uses six primary file types:

- A workbook file (.xlsx) contains individual worksheets, which can contain cell values, formulas, formatting information, styles, graphics, drawing objects, hyperlinks, charts, and data validation settings. Files saved using the default .xlsx format cannot contain macros. You can open and edit files in other formats, such as text files (.txt), Excel files created using previous program versions (.xls), and Access database tables, but those files will not have all of the built-in functionality that comes with Excel. You can, of course, save Excel workbooks in any of the aforementioned formats—and more.

NOTE

Excel 97–2003 could open Lotus 1-2-3 files, but Excel 2007 no longer supports files created using that program.

- A macro-enabled workbook (.xlsm) file is the same as a standard workbook (.xlsx) file, except that it enables you to record macros that you can replay to repeat a procedure without going through the individual steps again. Excel records its macros in the Visual Basic for Applications (VBA) programming language, which lets programmers make changes to the computers where the macro file resides. Evildoers write viruses and other harmful programs using VBA, so Microsoft changed the Excel 2007 file formats and macro security settings to help prevent malicious software from infecting your computer. Excel 2007 will only run macros if they are contained in a workbook of the proper type (.xlsm or .xls), and you give Excel permission to run the macro.

- A template (.xltx) file holds all of the information that a standard workbook file contains, plus styles formatting and other settings that have been applied. For example, if you create a workbook to record monthly expenses in three categories, you can lay out all the elements and save it as a template. When you base a new file on a template, you get the headings, instructions, formatting, and so on that you created previously—a blank boilerplate that can now hold fresh data. (Just remember to save your work as an .xlsx file.)

- Just as template (.xltx) files enable you to create standard (.xlsx) workbooks, macro-enabled templates (.xltm) let you create identical copies of macro-enabled workbooks (.xlsm).

- A workspace file (.xlw) contains pointers to other Excel files that you had open during a session. When you open a workspace file, Excel opens all the other Excel files it refers to. Workspace files are particularly useful if you frequently work with the same set of files and need to have them all open at once.

- If the AutoRecover feature is on (Office Button → Excel Options), click the Save category, and check the "Save AutoRecover info every x minutes" box. Excel creates a quick backup of your work periodically. AutoRecover will often get most, if not all, of your data back in the event of a crash, but it's no substitute for clicking the Save button frequently. You can find where each version of Excel saves its AutoRecover files, along with other default file locations, in Chapter 3.

TIP

The best time to save a workbook is after you have done something you would hate to have to do again, which means that clicking the Save button should become a reflex. Don't rely on AutoRecover to save your work for you!

Tips on Using Templates

- Always save your templates in the default Excel template folder. If you installed Office 2007 on your *C:* drive and didn't change any folder settings, that folder is *C:\ Documents and Settings\username\Application Data\ Microsoft\Templates*. In that directory path, the string *username* represents the name of the Windows account you're currently using. Saving templates in that folder causes the templates to appear in the New Workbook dialog box when you click Office Button → New, and then click the My Templates category header.

- When you create a workbook from a template, you create a new workbook based on the template. However, if you use the Open dialog box to open the template file, you will be editing the template.

- Right-click a template, click New, and you will create a new workbook based on the template.

- To create a template for a worksheet, delete all but one worksheet in a workbook, apply the desired settings (formats, styles, repeating rows and columns, etc.), and save the workbook as a template (.xltx file for normal workbooks or .xltm file for macro-enabled workbooks).

- The templates available in the Spreadsheet Solutions section of the Templates dialog box are formatted for common business uses, such as time cards, balance sheets, expense reports, purchase orders, and sales invoices. (To display the templates, click Office Button → New, and click the Installed Templates category heading.)

TIP

If you click Office Button → New and click the Installed Templates category header, Excel displays the same templates you'll see if you were to right-click a sheet tab, click Insert, and click the Spreadsheet Solutions tab. The difference between the two operations is that the former procedure creates a new workbook, while the latter adds the template's worksheets to your existing workbook.

The Anatomy of an Excel File

Think of an Excel file as a collection of data about a given topic, such as sales revenue or time spent on projects. For example, if you were keeping track of your billable hours on a series of projects and had to submit your hours each week, you could create a workbook representing a year and use each worksheet to record your hours per week. You would need to add worksheets for each week (a workbook's default is three), but the grouping would make sense. If your company maintained a quarterly billing cycle, you could also keep your hours in workbooks of only 13 worksheets, each representing a week in a fiscal quarter.

A Workbook

While an Excel workbook appears to be a single entity, there are actually three different layers: the data layer (the ground floor of your document that holds the worksheet data, formulas, and so on); a back drawing layer (the basement, where you can put background images, such as wallpaper or different colors that make the data easier to read); and a top drawing layer (the second floor, where you can add graphics to highlight important data, or display comments in a text box). Figure 1-8 illustrates how the three layers interact within a workbook.

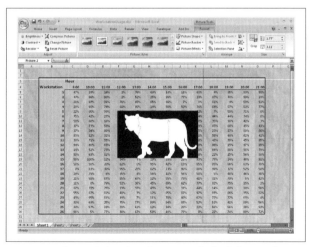

Figure 1-8. This worksheet has elements in the back drawing layer, data layer, and top drawing layer.

The lines in the background of the sheet are repetitions of a texture graphic, while the image of a tiger is a clip art file. The contents on a higher drawing layer obscure the contents of a lower layer. In Figure 1-8, the picture of the tiger obscures data contained in the worksheet's cells; in turn, the cell data obscures the background pattern.

A Worksheet

In Excel, worksheets are where the rubber meets the road; worksheets hold your data, formulas, images, and formatting. Worksheets are tables made up of columns and rows—you can identify a cell in an Excel worksheet based on its column (which are lettered) and its row (which are numbered, e.g., A5).

TIP

If you would rather refer to a cell's address only by numbers, use "R1C1" notation, where the row is preceded by the letter "R", and the column is preceded by the letter "C". R1C1 refers to cell A1, R2C2 to cell B2, and so on.

To see your formulas in R1C1 reference format, click Office Button → Excel Options, click the Formulas category header, and check the R1C1 Reference Style box.

Sheet Tabs

The sheet tabs, found on the tab bar at the lower left of the Excel window (Figure 1-9), don't get a lot of attention. But the sheet tabs (and the tab bar) are useful for organizing and customizing your workbooks. You can change the order of the worksheets by dragging a worksheet tab to the desired spot. Right-click a sheet tab and from the shortcut menu you can rename the worksheet and change other attributes.

Figure 1-9. The tab bar lets you manage the worksheets in your workbook.

You can change the color of a sheet tab, which makes it easy to identify individual worksheets, such as a worksheet where you changed some values. It's also a handy organizational tool—you could, for example, color code tabs by fiscal quarter.

TIP

A lot of people concentrate on organizing data within a worksheet and forget how the worksheets fit within the workbook as a whole. Use the sheet tabs and the tab bar to organize data by category.

Formatting

The data and formulas that fill a workbook are, ultimately, the most important part of your work with Excel, but how you present your data can make the difference between an easily understood summary and a difficult slog through a twisty maze of numbers. Each workbook element has formatting characteristics that you can change to maximize the effectiveness of your information.

Worksheets

Compared to the other elements of a workbook, there are very few formatting options you can apply to a worksheet as a whole. You can change the margins (Page Layout → Margins), or add a header and footer to a worksheet. As shown in Figure 1-10, a header is a block of space reserved at the top of a page, while a footer is a block of space reserved at the bottom of a page. The text in a header and footer—the date, your company name, etc.—repeats on every printed page of the worksheet they're attached to. To display the "Header and Footer" dialog box, click Insert → Header and Footer, add custom text, or include AutoText entries such as the time, date, page number, and total number of pages for the worksheet. You can also include images in a header or footer.

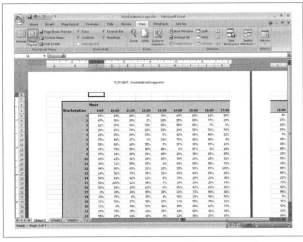

Figure 1-10. A header and footer repeat information, such as page numbers and dates, on each printed page.

In a similar vein, you can repeat column and row titles on subsequent pages. Click the Page Layout tab, click the Page Setup group's dialog expander, and then click Sheet to display the Sheet tab of the Page Setup dialog box. Using the "Rows to Repeat at Top" and "Columns to Repeat at Left" controls, you can select the titles you want to appear on each page. If you're printing a worksheet that requires two or more pages, strongly consider repeating the row and column headers on each page.

Just remember that setting rows and columns to repeat on each *printed* page doesn't help as you scroll through a worksheet. Scroll far enough and those headings will disappear. You can freeze rows and columns so they remain visible as you scroll through a worksheet by clicking the cell below and to the right of the rows and columns you want to remain constant, clicking View → Freeze Panes, and selecting whether to freeze rows and columns based on the current selection, freeze just the first row, or freeze just the first column. You can return your worksheet to normal by clicking View → Freeze Panes → Unfreeze Panes.

TIP

Freezing panes has no effect on how the worksheet is printed. Using the controls on the Sheet page of the Page Setup dialog box has no impact on your worksheet as you view it in the Excel window.

One of the toughest decisions when formatting a worksheet's contents is to determine the appearance of each element. Data labels, headings, and the data itself must be formatted. There is a lot to keep track of, but Excel 2007 comes with a wide array of Office Themes you can apply to your workbooks. To see how an Office Theme affects your worksheet's appearance, click Page Layout → Themes, and then hover your mouse pointer over the theme you'd like to apply. Even if there isn't an Office Theme to your liking, you can change the colors, fonts, and text effects in an existing theme and save it as a new theme for later use.

Finally, if you want to hide one or more worksheets in your workbook, simply click its tab, then click Home → Format → Hide & Unhide → Hide Sheet. To unhide it, click Home → Format → Hide & Unhide → Unhide Sheet, and select the worksheet to reveal from the Unhide dialog box. Hiding a worksheet is not a good way to secure its contents, but it's an easy way to direct attention to the worksheets you want your colleagues to notice.

Columns and Rows

The highest level of organization within a worksheet is the column and the row. Columns are vertical collections of cells, and each column is designated by a letter. Rows are horizontal and are designated by a number. The standard column is 56 pixels wide, and the standard row is 16 pixels high—tall and wide enough to hold a little over eight characters in the default 9-point Calibri font.

TIP

A pixel is a dot on your computer screen, so the amount of space a row or column takes up on your screen depends on the size and resolution of your monitor.

You can change the height of a row or the width of a column by dragging a border of the row or column header until it is the desired size. Excel displays the current width or height of the row or column as you drag the border, so you can make precise changes. If you would rather type in a value instead of dragging, click a cell, then click Home → Format → Column Width, and type in the new width (in numbers—a width of 9 will hold 9 digits, but maybe only 5 *w*s or 12 *i*s). To adjust row height, click Home → Format → Row Height, and type in the new height.

You can even tell Excel to change the row height or column width to reflect the row's or column's contents. Clicking Home → Format → AutoFit Column Width, or Home → Format → AutoFit Row Height tells Excel to make the selected row or column just big enough to display the contents of the widest and tallest cells in that row or column.

It's easy to think of the rows and columns of a worksheet as fixed, but you can always insert or delete a column or row. To insert a column, click Home → Insert → Insert Sheet Columns; columns are added to the left of the column with the active cell. To insert a row, click Home → Insert → Insert Sheet Rows; rows are added above the row with the active cell. Excel updates all of your formulas automatically to reflect the referenced cells' new positions in the workbook, so adding rows or columns won't introduce any errors. Deleting rows and columns is just as straightforward—right-click the row or column header and click Delete.

Just as you can hide and unhide worksheets, you can hide or unhide rows and columns. Simply right-click the row or column header and click Hide. To unhide a row or column, you need to select the row or column headers on either side (e.g., select the headers of rows 1 and 3 if row 2 is hidden), and click Home → Format → Hide & Unhide → Unhide Rows, or Home → Format → Hide & Unhide → Unhide Columns.

If you want to change the appearance of every cell in a row or column, click the column or row header and use the controls on the Home tab (or the controls in the Format Cells dialog box) to set data type, alignment, font, size, style, borders, and more.

Cells

The smallest unit of organization in a worksheet is the cell, which is formed by the intersection of a row and a column. Changing the appearance of individual cells is exactly the same as changing the formatting of a column or row—you select the cells and use the controls on the Home tab of the Ribbon or in the Format Cells dialog box. You can find most of the available cell formatting options on the Home tab, but the Format Cells dialog box offers further possibilities (see Figure 1-11).

Two useful formatting options are controlled by checkboxes in the Text Control section of the Alignment tab: "Wrap text" and "Shrink to fit". The first forces text in a cell to fit within the left and right borders of a cell. The cell will expand vertically to accommodate its contents. "Shrink to fit" does the opposite, reducing text size until it fits within the cell.

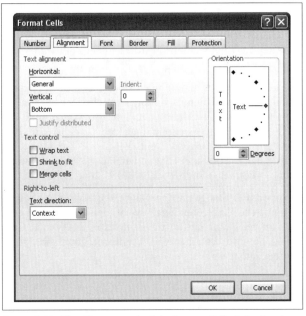

Figure 1-11. The Alignment tab of the Format Cells dialog box lets you control the orientation of text in your cells.

TIP

"Shrink to fit" and "Wrap text" are mutually exclusive; selecting "Wrap text" disables the "Shrink to fit" checkbox, and vice versa.

Finally, just as you can insert and delete columns, you can insert and delete cells. Since inserting or deleting cells can shift the surrounding cells, you can select the direction in which surrounding worksheet cells are pushed. If you add cells, Excel will adjust any existing formulas that reference cells that were moved. If you delete a cell that's used in a formula, however, the formula will generate an error. You'll have to edit the formula to reference the appropriate cells.

Characters

When you want to change the appearance of a cell's contents, you just select the cell and have at it. Editing individual characters in a cell isn't obvious—click the cell and select the characters you want to format in the formula bar at the top of the worksheet (Figure 1-12) or inside the cell itself. The formatting controls on the Home tab of the Ribbon and the Format Cells dialog box are, as always, at your disposal.

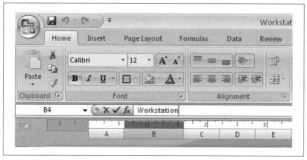

Figure 1-12. Edit a cell's contents either in the cell or the formula bar.

Formatting applied to individual characters overrides formatting applied to the cell as a whole.

Styles

A style is a prefab format, from alignment to font to borders, that you can apply to a cell. Like Word 2007, Excel 2007 has a substantially larger set of built-in styles than was available in previous versions of Office. To see which styles are available, click Home → Cell Styles, and select from among the different offerings that appear in the Cell Styles gallery (see Figure 1-13).

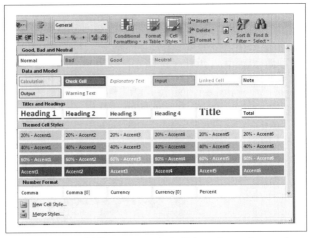

Figure 1-13. Excel 2007 presents the built-in styles, and any styles you've created, in the Cell Styles gallery.

You can, of course, create your own custom cell styles. To do so, click Home → Cell Styles → New Cell Style to display the Style dialog box, shown in Figure 1-14.

When you display the Style dialog box, it shows the details of the style that's applied to the active cell. When you view a style in here, you see a series of checkboxes indicating how various elements (alignment, font, border, etc.) are formatted in the style. To view the details of a style, click the Format button, which displays all the tabs in the Format Cells dialog box. At this point, you can flip through the tabs and change any element, from font size to disabling protection.

To delete a style, right-click it in the Cell Styles gallery and click Delete. If you'd like to modify an existing style, right-click the style in the Cell Styles gallery and click Modify to display the Style dialog box. As when you create a new style, clicking the Format button in the Style dialog box displays the Format Cells dialog box, which you can use to change the selected format.

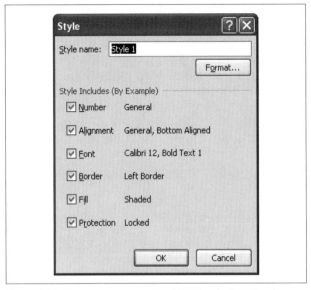

Figure 1-14. You can create new Excel 2007 styles by using the controls in the Style dialog box.

Shortcut Menus and the Mini Toolbar

One handy Windows tool is the right-click menu. Right-clicking an object in a program (such as a cell, row or column header, or sheet tab) displays a short menu of commonly used commands. Microsoft calls these shortcut menus *context menus*. Figure 1-15 shows the shortcut menu that appears when you right-click a cell.

Here is a quick summary of Excel's right-click talents:

- Right-clicking a cell displays a shortcut menu with a formatting toolbar you can use to format the cell quickly; editing commands that let you paste, cut, copy, or paste a special item (such as a picture or another workbook) into the cell; commands that let you delete, insert, or

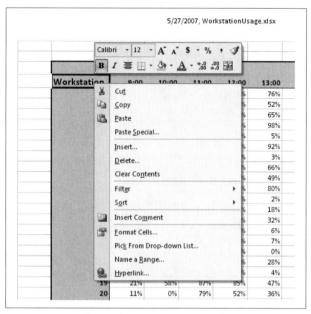

Figure 1-15. Excel 2007 shortcut menus contain buttons and menu items.

clear the contents of the cell; attach a comment; change the cell's format using the Format Cells dialog box; input a value that already exists in the column; filter or sort worksheet values based on other values in the cell's column; define the cell as part of a named range; and create a hyperlink.

- Right-clicking a row or column header displays a shortcut menu that contains commands to format the object you right-clicked; cut, copy, paste, and paste special; insert, delete, or clear the contents of the row or column; display the Format Cells dialog box; change the row's height or the column's width; as well as options to hide or unhide the row or column.

- Right-clicking a sheet tab lets you insert a new worksheet; delete, rename, hide, move, or copy the sheet you right-clicked; select all sheets; change the worksheet's tab color; or view the code of any macros attached to the sheet.

- Right-clicking a drawing object lets you format the object quickly using controls on a formatting toolbar; cut, copy, or paste the object; edit the object's text; change the object's appearance, size, grouping, and ordering; assign a hyperlink or macro to the object; and assign the shape as the default shape for that workbook.

- Right-clicking a Ribbon button lets you add the button to the Quick Access Toolbar. Similarly, right-clicking a Ribbon group's name bar (e.g., the Page Setup tab's Themes group) lets you add the group to the Quick Access Toolbar.

- Right-clicking a button on the Quick Access Toolbar lets you remove the button from the Quick Access Toolbar, customize the Quick Access Toolbar, display the Quick Access Toolbar below the Ribbon (making the Quick Access Toolbar larger), or minimize the Ribbon.

- Right-clicking the status bar (at the very bottom of the window) lets you change the summary operations.

Excel 2007's shortcut menus have a new item at the top: the Mini Toolbar, which is a small toolbar that contains buttons for the most commonly used formatting commands (e.g., font, font size, font color, fill color, bold, italic, center, etc.). The Mini Toolbar also appears when you select a group of cells and hover your mouse pointer over the selection. Excel 2007 initially draws the Mini Toolbar faintly, but makes it more prominent as you move your mouse pointer closer to it.

How Excel Tries to Help

Excel has a lot going on (you can decide whether that means Excel is "feature rich" or "bloated"), and it should make your life easier. And it does, with several automated features. One useful task Excel performs in the background is saving AutoRecover information—worksheet data, macros, formulas, etc.—so if the program crashes, you lose as little work as possible. There are three other things Excel does in the background (AutoCorrect, AutoComplete, and Smart Tags), but you can turn these—and AutoRecover—off if you wish.

TIP

One thing Excel doesn't do automatically is highlight suspected spelling and grammar errors in your worksheet. To check spelling, click Review → Spelling.

AutoCorrect

People make the same spelling mistakes again and again, usually those little transpositions ("adn" for "and") that drive you crazy. Don't fret. Excel has this and other common misspellings in its list terms to correct automatically.

TIP

If Excel makes a change you don't want, you can undo the change by pressing Ctrl-Z or clicking the Undo button on the Quick Access Toolbar.

You can add, remove, or redefine AutoCorrect entries by clicking Office Button → Excel Options, clicking the Proofing category head, and then clicking the AutoCorrect Options button. In the dialog box, you can select the types of changes Excel can make or, by unchecking the "Replace text as you type" box, prevent Excel from making any corrections automatically. To add an entry, type the text in the Replace field and the text to replace it in the With field.

If you type in the same lengthy phrases frequently, save your fingers.

You can define an AutoCorrect entry that inserts your boilerplate text whenever you type several letters of the phrase (such as "vty" for "very truly yours").

Excel also recognizes web addresses and network paths, and automatically formats them as hyperlinks. Excel 2007 also determines whether your entry should be added to an existing Excel table. You can control these options on the "Auto-Format as You Type" tab.

AutoComplete

Most Excel users often enter the same data in a worksheet. For example, if you keep your business' customer data in a worksheet, many of your customers will probably be from the same state. Excel recognizes repeated values in a column and offers to fill in the expected value. You can turn Auto-Complete on by clicking Office Button → Excel Options, clicking the Advanced category head, and then, in the Editing Options section at the top of the dialog box, checking the "Enable AutoComplete for Cell Values" box.

Smart Tags

Another way Excel automates operations is with Smart Tags. Excel 2007 recognizes specific data in a cell (be it a stock quote or the address of a recently sent email), and tags the cell with a tiny purple notch in the lower-right corner. To turn on Smart Tags, click Office Button → Excel Options, click the Proofing category head, click the Smart Tags tab, and then check the "Label data with smart tags" box.

To test how Smart Tags work, turn them on—enter a stock symbol, for example—hover the pointer over the notch, and then click the Smart Tags action button. You can use the options displayed to summon a fresh quote, a company report on MSN, and more.

NOTE

You can find more Smart Tags on the Microsoft web site by clicking the More Smart Tags button.

CHAPTER 2

Excel Tasks

This chapter gives you quick answers about how to perform common and essential tasks in Excel. You'll find information on tasks that are new to you, and you'll save time on tasks you already know. The tasks are divided into the following categories:

- Working with files
- Printing
- Moving around in a workbook or worksheet
- Manipulating workbooks and worksheets
- Manipulating rows, columns, and cells
- Entering and editing data
- Formatting cells
- Working with hyperlinks
- Working with headers and footers
- Summarizing data
- Using named ranges
- Defining alternative data sets
- Controlling how data is displayed
- Protecting all or part of a workbook
- Spelling and other tools
- Customizing Excel
- Collaborating
- Working with the Web

- Summarizing data with charts
- Analyzing data with PivotTables and PivotCharts

Working with Files

Use the following answers to help you create, find, save, preview, and set the properties of Excel files.

How do I...

Create a new workbook without starting Excel?
> Right-click any blank space in a folder or desktop and select New → Microsoft Excel Worksheet.

Create a new workbook within Excel?
> Press Ctrl-N or click Office Button → New, then double-click Blank Workbook under the "Blank and Recent" section.

Create a workbook from a template?
> Click Office Button → New; in the Templates pane, click the category of template you want to display, and then double-click the template on which you want to base your workbook.

Open a workbook?
> Click Office Button → Open or press Ctrl-O; navigate to the file you want to open. Optionally, you can click the down arrow on the Open dialog box's Open button to open the workbook in different ways (read-only, in a web browser, etc.).

NOTE

In Excel 2002 and 2003, you could search for a file from within Excel. That capability doesn't exist in Excel 2007, so you must use the Windows operating system's Search feature. To search for a file in Windows, click the Start Button → Search, and use the controls in the Search dialog box to find the file you want.

Save a workbook?

Click the Save button on the Quick Access Toolbar, press Ctrl-S, or Office Button → Save. Click Office Button → Save As to save a workbook under a different name, in a different location, or as a different file type. Enter the name of the new file, navigate to the directory folder where you want to save the file, and click Save.

Save a workbook as a web page?

Click Office Button → Save As to display the Save As dialog box. Type a name for the web page in the File name box, click the "Save as type" down arrow, and then click Web Page (*.htm; *.html). Click the Entire Workbook or Selection option button to indicate which part(s) of the workbook you want to save, and then click the Save button.

Save all open workbooks as a workspace?

Click View → Save Workspace. If you open the workspace file, Excel will open all the workbooks you had open when you created the workspace.

Change the summary information of a workbook?

Click Office Button → Prepare → Properties, and enter new information in the appropriate fields.

Set the custom properties of a workbook?

Click Office Button → Prepare → Properties, click the Document Properties down arrow, and then click Advanced Properties. In the Properties dialog box, click the Custom tab; select the properties to add, and enter the desired values.

Save a preview picture with a workbook?

Click Office Button → Prepare → Properties, click the Document Properties down arrow, and then click Advanced Properties. In the Properties dialog box, click the Summary tab, and then check the "Save preview picture" box.

Change the number of recently used files that appear on the File menu?

Click Office Button → Excel Options, click the Advanced category header, and in the Display group, in the "Show this number of Recent Documents" box, type the number of files to appear (50 is the limit). To display no recently used files, type **0**.

Set the default file location?

Click Office Button → Excel Options, click the Save category header, and type the desired location in the Default file location box.

Prevent personal information from being saved with a workbook created in Excel 2007?

Click Office Button → Excel Options, click the Trust Center category header, click the Trust Center Settings button, click the Privacy Options category header, and then click the Document Inspector button. If prompted to save your workbook, click Yes. In the Document Inspector dialog box, check the boxes representing the types of content for which you want to scan, and then click Inspect. The Document Inspector dialog box displays Remove All buttons in the categories where it found the specified content types. Click the appropriate Remove All button to delete that type of content from your file; click Close when you're done.

Keep personal information from being saved with a workbook created in an earlier version of Excel?

Click Office Button → Excel Options, click the Trust Center category header, click the Trust Center Settings button, click the Privacy Options category header, and then check the "Remove personal information from this file on save" box.

Recover a workbook after Excel crashes?

Start Excel. When Excel starts, it recovers as much of the file as it can.

Change how often Excel saves AutoRecover information?

Click Office Button → Excel Options, click the Save tab, and set the "Save AutoRecover information every xx minutes" box.

Change the location where Excel saves AutoRecover information?

Click Office Button → Excel Options, click the Save tab and change the path in the "AutoRecover file location" field.

Start Excel in safe mode?

Press Ctrl when you start Excel or type **excel.exe /safe** at a Windows command prompt (in Windows, click Start → Run). When you start Excel in safe mode, all nonessential elements, such as add-ins and the Auto-Correct list, are not loaded.

Enable items disabled during a start in safe mode?

Click Office Button → Excel Options, and click the Add-Ins category header. On the Manage menu, click Disabled Items and then click Go. In the Disabled Items dialog box, select the items you want to use and click the Enable button.

Printing

Use the following answers to help you print entire workbooks, individual worksheets, parts of worksheets, and more.

How do I…

Print a single copy of the active worksheet without using the Print dialog box?
> Click Office Button → Print → Quick Print or Ctrl-P.

Set the print area of a worksheet?
> Select the cells you want to print and click Page Layout → Print Area → Set Print Area.

NOTE

Excel 2007 checks for blank cells at the bottom and right edge of a print area and eliminates them automatically so you don't print any pages with empty cells.

Set the print area of multiple worksheets?
> Select the sheet tabs of the worksheets for which you want to set the print area. Then, on the active worksheet, select the cells you want to print and click Page Layout → Print Area → Set Print Area.

Print an entire worksheet even if it has a defined print area?
> Click Office Button → Print, and in the "Print what" section, check the "Ignore print areas" box.

Set a print area made up of discontiguous cells?
> Select the first group of cells you want to print, then hold down Ctrl and select the next groups of cells, and click Page Layout → Print Area → Set Print Area.

Remove a print area?
> Click Page Layout → Print Area → Clear Print Area.

View how my worksheet will appear when it's printed?
> Click View → Page Layout.

Preview what I am about to print?
> Click Office Button → Print → Print Preview.

Preview where the page breaks occur in what I am about to print?

Click View → Page Break Preview. You can drag the page breaks to new locations in the Page Break Preview window (Figure 2-1).

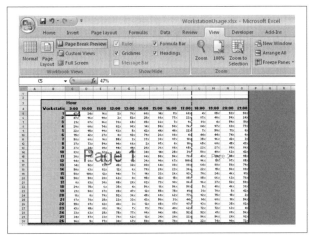

Figure 2-1. Set page breaks for a worksheet in the Page Break Preview window.

Print a range of pages of a worksheet?

Click Office Button → Print, and in the Print range section, enter the first and last page you want to print in the From and To boxes.

Print every worksheet in a workbook?

Click Office Button → Print and select Entire Workbook in the "Print what" area.

Print selected worksheets in a workbook?

Hold down Ctrl when you click the tabs of the worksheets you want to print; click Office Button → Print. ("Active Sheets" will be selected in the Print what area.)

Print selected cells on the active worksheet?
> Select the cells you want to print; click Office Button → Print and check Selection.

Print one or more workbooks from Windows?
> Select the workbooks you want to print in Windows Explorer, right-click, and click Print. Windows will launch Excel, print the selected workbooks, and close Excel with no further action from you.

Print to a file?
> Click Office Button → Print; check the "Print to file" box, click OK, and supply a file name.

Print more than one copy?
> Click Office Button → Print and set value in "Number of copies" field.

Collate the pages of the multiple copies?
> Click Office Button → Print and check the Collate box.

Set your printer's options?
> Click Office Button → Print and click the Properties button.

Change the orientation of the printed page?

 Click Office Button → Print, then click the Properties button → Layout; choose Portrait, Landscape, or Rotated Landscape. Or, click Page Layout → Orientation and choose Portrait or Landscape.

Change the scale of printing?
> Click Page Layout and then, in the "Scale to fit" group, change the value in the Scale box.

Fit the printout on a set number of pages?
> Click Page Layout and then, in the "Scale to fit" group, set the values in the Width and Height list boxes.

Change the margins of a workbook?

Click Page Layout → Margins, and either click a built-in margin setting or click Custom Margins to display the Margins tab of the Page Setup dialog box. On the Margins tab, enter the amount of blank space you want around the page.

Repeat rows at the top of a printed page?

Click Page Layout → Print Titles to display the Page Setup dialog box's Sheet tab. In the "Rows to repeat at top" field, click the button on the right and select the row headers you want to repeat. Click the button again, and then click OK.

Repeat columns at the left of a printed page?

Click Page Layout → Print Titles to display the Page Setup dialog box's Sheet tab. In the "Columns to repeat at left" field, click the button on the right inside the field and select the column headers you want to repeat. Click the button again, and then click OK.

Print gridlines?

Click the Page Layout tab and then, in the Sheet Options group, check the Gridlines Print box.

Print a worksheet in black and white?

On the Page Layout tab, click the Page Setup group's dialog expander. In the Page Setup dialog box, click the Sheet tab, and check the "Black and white" box.

Print a worksheet in draft quality?

On the Page Layout tab, click the Page Setup group's dialog expander. In the Page Setup dialog box, click the Sheet tab, and check the "Draft quality" box.

Print worksheet comments?

On the Page Layout tab, click the Page Setup group's dialog expander. In the Page Setup dialog box, click the Sheet tab. In the Comments pull-down menu, select whether to print the comments at the end of the worksheet or in the body of the worksheet.

Print error codes?

On the Page Layout tab, click the Page Setup group's dialog expander. In the Page Setup dialog box, click the Sheet tab, click the "Cell errors as" down arrow, and select how you want the errors represented in your printed worksheet.

Change the order in which pages are printed?

On the Page Layout tab, click the Page Setup group's dialog expander. In the Page Setup dialog box, click the Sheet tab. In the "Page order" area, click the "Down, then over" or the "Over, then down" option.

Moving Around in a Workbook or Worksheet

Use the following answers to help you navigate in workbooks and worksheets.

How do I…

Move from one worksheet to another?

Click the sheet tab at the bottom of the screen representing the worksheet you want, or Press Ctrl-PgDn to select the next sheet, and Ctrl-PgUp to select the previous sheet.

Scroll around in a worksheet?

Click the arrows in the vertical scroll bar to move up or down through a worksheet. Click the arrows in the horizontal scroll bar to move left or right. You can also drag the scroll handle on either scroll bar to move quickly through your worksheet. Changing the view of your worksheet using the scroll bars does not change the active cell.

Hide the scroll bars?

Click Office Button → Excel Options, click the Advanced category header, and scroll to the "Display options for this workbook" section. Uncheck the "Show horizontal scroll bar" and "Show vertical scroll bar" boxes.

Move around a worksheet using the keyboard?

The Up, Down, Left, and Right arrows will move the active cell in the respective direction. Tab moves the active cell one column to the right. Shift-Tab moves the active cell one column to the left. Pressing Enter moves the active cell down one row; Shift-Enter moves it one row up.

NOTE

For a complete list of movement keys, see Chapter 4.

Change the default movement of the Enter key?

Click Office Button → Excel Options, click the Advanced category header. In the "Editing options" section, check the "After pressing Enter, move selection" box, then open the Direction pull-down menu and select the direction you want.

Go to a specific place in a workbook?

Click Home → Find & Select → Go To, or Ctrl-G or F5. Select or type in the cell or range you want to move to (such as a named range) and click OK.

Control which items are displayed in the Go To dialog box?

Click Home → Find & Select → Go To Special, and select the items to show.

Find text in a worksheet?

Click Home → Find & Select → Find or Ctrl-F. Enter the text to find in the dialog box. Click the Find Next button. Click the Options button to display more ways to search for text in your worksheet. With the extra options displayed, open the Within pull-down menu on the Find tab and select "Workbook" to search all the sheets in your workbook. Click Find All to list all occurrences at the bottom of the "Find and Replace" dialog box. Click an instance in this list to highlight the cell containing the text.

Make a find operation case-sensitive?

Click Home → Find & Select → Find or Ctrl-F, click the Options button, and check the "Match case" box.

Find text based on the entire value in a cell?

Click Home → Find & Select → Find or Ctrl-F, click the Options button, and check the "Find entire cells only" box.

Find text in formulas, cell values, or comments?

Click Home → Find & Select → Find or Ctrl-F, click the Options button, and select the cell attribute in the "Look in" pull-down menu.

Change the search order?

Click Home → Find & Select → Find or Ctrl-F, click the Options button, and select either By Row or By Column in the "Look in" pull-down menu.

Find text with a specific format?

Click Home → Find & Select → Find or Ctrl-F, click the Options button, then the Format button. In the Find Format dialog box, pick the formats you want to search for or click the "Choose Format from Cell" button, and then click any cell with the format you want to find.

TIP

If you put any temporary or placeholder values in a worksheet, always give them a unique format (red text, italics, etc.). Before you use a worksheet in a report, use Find Format to scan the worksheet for data that must be verified or updated.

Find and replace text in a worksheet?

Click Home → Find & Select → Replace or Ctrl-H. Enter the text to find in the "Find what" field; enter the text to replace it in the "Replace with" field. Click the Find Next button to highlight the next occurrence in your worksheet, and click the Replace button. Click the Find All button to list all occurrences at the bottom of the "Find and Replace" dialog box. Click the Replace All button to replace every instance of the text in the "Find what" field (Figure 2-2).

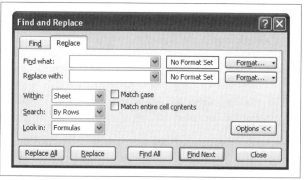

Figure 2-2. The "Find and Replace" dialog box lets you search for text with specific formatting.

Find and replace specific formatting?

Home → Find & Select → Replace or Ctrl-H. Click the Options button, then the Format button next to the Find what field. Select the formats to find and click OK. Click the Format button next to the "Replace with" field and define the formats you want to replace them with.

Manipulating Workbooks and Worksheets

Use the following answers to add, delete, or rearrange the worksheets in your workbooks.

How do I…

Add a worksheet?

Click Home → Insert → Insert Sheet. The worksheet appears in front of the active worksheet. You can also right-click a sheet tab, click Insert, and double-click Worksheet.

Delete a worksheet?

Right-click the sheet tab and click Delete, or use Home → Delete → Delete Sheet.

Move a worksheet?

Click the tab and drag. Or right-click the sheet tab and click Move or Copy. Open the To Book menu to move the sheet to a different workbook (or a new workbook).

To move the sheet within the same workbook, select its place in the "Before sheet" list.

Copy a worksheet?

Ctrl-click the sheet tab, drag it to the new place, release the mouse button, then release Ctrl. Or right-click the sheet tab and click Move or Copy. Check the Create a copy box, open the To Book menu, and select the workbook (or a new workbook).

NOTE

If you're setting up a workbook where all the worksheets will have the same structure, format one worksheet the way you want it, then create copies of it.

Rename a worksheet?

Right-click the sheet tab, click Rename, and type in a new name. Or select Home → Format → Rename Sheet.

Reorder worksheets?

Drag the sheet tab into a new position on the tab bar. As you drag the tab, a black triangle marks where the worksheet would be placed if you released the mouse button.

Change the default number of worksheets in a workbook?

Click Office Button → Excel Options, click the Popular category header (if necessary), and change the number in the "Include this many sheets" field. The maximum is 255 sheets.

Change the color of a sheet tab?

Right-click the sheet tab, click Tab Color, and pick the color in the palette that appears; or click Home → Format → Tab Color and pick the desired color.

Manipulating Rows, Columns, and Cells

Use these answers to change the layout of an individual worksheet by adding, deleting, and moving cells, rows, and columns.

How do I...

Insert cells into a worksheet?

Click the cell where you want to insert a new cell and click Home → Insert → Insert Cells. Pick which way the surrounding cells should shift and click OK.

Insert a block of cells into a worksheet?

Select a group of cells in the shape of the desired insertion and click Home → Insert → Insert Cells; select the option button indicating the direction you want the surrounding cells to shift.

Insert a column?

Click any cell in the column to the right of where you want the new column to appear; click Home → Insert → Insert Sheet Columns.

Insert a row?

Click any cell in the row below where you want the new row to appear; click Home → Insert → Insert Sheet Rows.

Use the Insert Options button?

Click the Insert Options button and select the option button representing the formatting you want the inserted material to take on.

NOTE

The Insert Options button only appears when you insert cells, rows, or columns that contain formatting.

Hide the Insert Options button?

To make it disappear for this operation only, press Esc. To prevent it from appearing after you insert cells, rows, or columns, Office Button → Excel Options, click the Advanced category header, scroll down to the "Cut, copy, and paste" section, and uncheck the "Show Insert Options buttons" box.

Move a column?

Select the column, right-click, and click Cut. Click any cell in the column to the right of where you want the moved column to appear; right-click and click Home → Insert → Insert Cut Cells. You can also Shift-drag the border of the column to the new place.

Move a row?

Select the row you want to move and click Cut. Click any cell in the row below where you want the moved row to appear; click Home → Insert → Insert Cut Cells. You can also Shift-drag the border of the row to the new place.

Delete cells from a worksheet?

Select the cells and click Home → Delete → Delete Cells; select the direction the surrounding cells should shift.

Delete a column?

Select the column(s); right-click in the selected area and click Delete.

Delete a row?

Select the row(s); right-click in the selected area and click Delete.

Hide a row?

Select any cells in the row(s); click Home → Format → Hide & Unhide → Hide Rows.

Hide a column?

 Select any cells in the column(s); click Home → Format → Hide & Unhide → Hide Columns.

Unhide a row?

Select the rows above and below the hidden row(s); click Home → Format → Hide & Unhide → Unhide Rows.

Unhide a column?

Select the columns to the left and right of the hidden column(s); click Home → Format → Hide & Unhide → Unhide Columns.

Change a column's width?

Hover the mouse pointer over the edge of a column header. When the pointer changes to a double-headed horizontal arrow, drag the column edge to the desired width. The column's changing width appears as a ScreenTip while you drag. The column's width is expressed using two values: the number of digits in the standard font that the column can display, followed in parentheses by the column's width in pixels.

You can change a column's width to a specific value by right-clicking a column header, picking Column Width, and entering a value.

Change a row's height?

Hover the mouse over the edge of a row header. When the mouse pointer changes to a double-headed vertical arrow, drag the row edge to the desired height. The row's changing height appears as a ScreenTip while you drag. The height is expressed in points (there are 72 points per inch) and the number of pixels.

You can change a row's height to a specific value by right-clicking a row header, choosing Row Height, and entering a value expressed in points.

Autofit a column to its contents?
Click Home → Format → AutoFit Column Width, or double-click the right edge of the column header.

Autofit a row to its contents?
Click Home → Format → AutoFit Row Height, or double-click the bottom edge of the cell header.

Entering and Editing Data

Use the following answers to help you enter, edit, and validate data.

Entering Data Efficiently

How do I…

Change how the cursor moves after pressing Enter?
Click Office Button → Excel Options, click the Advanced category header. In the "Editing options" section, check the "After pressing Enter, move selection" box, then open the Direction pull-down menu and select the direction you want.

Use AutoComplete?
Click Office Button → Excel Options, click the Advance category header, and then, in the "Editing options" group, check the "Enable AutoComplete for cell values" box.

Turn off AutoComplete?
Uncheck the "Enable AutoComplete for cell values" box.

Pick a value from a list of values already appearing in the column?

Right-click the cell into which you want to enter the value, and select "Pick from Drop-down List". In the list that appears, select the item you want to enter into the cell.

Repeat the same value across a range of cells?

Select the cells into which you want to enter the value, type the value in the active cell, and press Ctrl-Enter.

Enter a carriage return in a cell?

 Press Alt-Enter.

Use Fill Series?

Type the first value of a series in a cell, type the second value of the series in a cell next to the original cell, select the cells, and drag the Fill Handle at the bottom-right corner of the active cell to the last cell you want included in the series.

The difference between the value in the first cell and the value in the second cell is the increment Excel uses to fill in the rest of the series. For example, the values 1 and 2 would result in the series of 1, 2, 3, 4..., while the values 1 and 3 would result in the series of 1, 3, 5, 7....

Change how dragging the Fill Handle extends a series?

Hold down the Ctrl key as you drag the Fill Handle. If dragging the Fill Handle would normally extend a series, Ctrl-dragging will repeat the selected values; if dragging the Fill Handle would normally repeat values, it will extend the series.

Use Fill Series with dates?

Type the first date in a cell, type the second date in a cell next to the original cell, and drag the Fill Handle at the bottom right of the active cell to the last cell you want included in the series.

Use Fill Series with days?

Type the first day (such as MON) in a cell and drag the Fill Handle at the bottom right of the active cell to the last cell you want included in the series.

You can skip days in the series by entering the appropriate values in the first two cells. For example, entering Monday and Wednesday would result in the series continuing Friday, Sunday, Tuesday, Thursday....

Use Fill Series with weekdays?

Type the first day (or date) of a series in the cell where you want the series to begin, type the second day of the series in a cell next to the original cell, right-mouse drag the fill handle, and select Fill Weekdays from the shortcut menu that appears when you release the mouse button.

Use Fill Series with months?

Type the first date in a cell, type the second day of the series in a cell next to the original cell and in the direction you want the series to progress, and drag the Fill Handle at the bottom right of the active cell to the last cell you want included in the series. Click the AutoFill Options button and select Fill Months. Or, right-drag the fill handle and select Fill Months from the shortcut menu that appears when you release the mouse button.

Use Fill Series with years?

Type the first date in a cell, type the second date in a cell next to the original cell, and drag the Fill Handle at the bottom right of the active cell to the last cell you want included in the series. Click the AutoFill Options button and select Fill Years. Or, right-drag the fill handle and select Fill Years from the shortcut menu that appears when you release the mouse button.

Use the AutoFill options button?

Click the AutoFill options button and select the option button representing the behavior you want the AutoFill operation to take on. You can fill the data according to the series established in the first two cells, copy the cells (repeating from the first cell if necessary), fill the data with the original formatting, or just fill the cells with the formats from the establishing cells.

Edit cell contents in the formula bar?

Click the cell you want to edit, click anywhere on the formula bar, and edit the text.

Allow editing within a cell?

Click Office Button → Excel Options, click the Advance category header, and then, in the "Editing options" group, check the "Allow editing directly in cells" box.

Create a data validation rule?

Click Data → Data Validation, click the Settings tab. Use the controls to select the type of data to accept and the rule to apply (Figure 2-3).

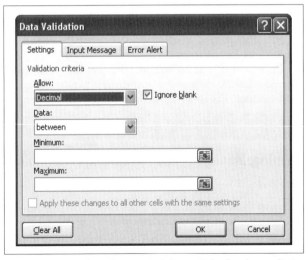

Figure 2-3. Controls in the Data Validation dialog box let you limit what data can be entered into a cell.

Require a user to enter data into a cell?

Click Data → Data Validation, then click the Settings tab. Select the type of data you'll allow in the cell and uncheck the Ignore Blank box.

Create custom messages explaining validation rules?

 Click Data → Data Validation, then click the Input Message tab. Type the message's title in the Title field, and the message in the Input Message box.

Create custom error messages when validation rules are violated?

Click Data → Data Validation, then click the Error Alert tab. Select the alert icon from the Style menu, type the title of the message and the message in the Input Message box.

Remove a data validation rule?

Click Data → Data Validation, then click the Clear All button.

Enter cell data by picking from a list?

Click Data → Data Validation, then click the Settings tab; select List from the Allow menu, click the button inside the Source field, and highlight the cells that contain the values to which you want to restrict the user. Click the button in the Data Validation field and click OK.

Creating, Managing, and Formatting Excel Tables

How do I...

Create an Excel table?

Type the headers and first row of data for your table into a worksheet, click any cell into which you entered data, click Home → Format as Table, and then click the format you want to apply to the table. In the "Format as Table" dialog box, verify that the "My table has headers" box is checked, and click OK.

Add data to an Excel table?

Click the cell at the bottom-right corner of the Excel table; press Tab to create a new table row. You may also type data into a cell in the row below the table's last row or to the right of the table's last column; Excel will expand the table to include the data.

Prevent table AutoExpansion?

To turn off table AutoExpansion, click Office Button Excel Options, click the Proofing category head, and click the AutoCorrect Options button. In the Auto-Correct dialog box, click the AutoFormat As You Type tab and clear the "Include new rows and columns in table" box. To undo a single instance of AutoExpansion, click the AutoCorrect Options button that appears after Excel adds a row or column to a table, and click Undo Table AutoExpansion.

TIP

You should always leave an empty column to the left and right of your table, and an empty row below your table, to ensure that Excel can reliably discern which cells belong to your table.

Resize an Excel table?

Drag the resizing handle at the bottom-right corner of the table to include the new columns and rows.

Delete Excel table columns?

Select the columns you want to delete, right-click any selected cell, and then click Delete → Table Columns.

Delete Excel table rows?

Select the rows you want to delete, right-click any selected cell, and then click Delete → Table Rows.

Convert an Excel table to a normal cell range?

Click any cell in your data list, click the Design contextual tab, and click "Convert to Range".

Add a Total row to an Excel table?

Click any cell in the Excel table, click the Design contextual tab, and check the Total Row box.

Change the summary function in a Total row cell?

Click the cell, click the down arrow, and then click the desired function. To select a function that's not on the list, click More Functions.

Apply an Excel table style?

Click any table cell, click the Design contextual tab, and click the style you want from the Table Styles gallery.

Turn banding on or off in an Excel table?

 Click any table cell, click the Design contextual tab, and check or clear the Banded Rows or Banded Columns boxes.

Create a new Excel table style?

Click any table cell, click the Design contextual tab, click the Table Styles gallery's More button, and then click New Table Style. In the New Table Quick Style dialog box (Figure 2-4), type a name for the new style, click the first table element you want to format, and click the Format button. Repeat the steps from within the New Table Quick Style dialog box until you've formatted all desired table elements.

Apply an Excel table style to a data list without creating a table?

Click any cell in your data list, click the Design contextual tab, and click the style you want from the Table Styles gallery. Then, on the Design contextual tab, click "Convert to Range".

Entering Data with a Data Entry Form

How do I...

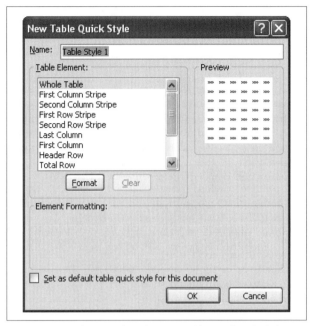

Figure 2-4. Use the controls in the New Table Quick Style dialog box to define a custom table style for your workbook.

Create a data entry form?

Right-click any spot on the Quick Access Toolbar and then click Customize Quick Access Toolbar. From the "Choose commands from" list box, select All Commands. In the Commands pane, click Form, and then click OK to display the Form button on the Quick Access Toolbar. Highlight the cells that contain the column labels of your list, or select one cell from the range that makes up your list and click the Form button. If necessary, click OK to accept the selected cells as the field labels for the form. If the labels are part of an existing list, the first record in the list will appear in the form.

Add a record to a list?

For a new data list, click Data → Form, and type the values for each column into the form. Press Tab to move from one form field to the next. If you press Tab while in the last form field, Excel will write the record to the list and create a new record. Pressing Enter adds whatever data you have entered to the list immediately, even if you haven't filled in every field.

Move to the previous record?

Click the Find Prev button.

Move to the next record?

Click the Find Next button.

Edit a record?

Display the record in the form, edit the values in the fields, and click the New button.

Undo all edits to a record before you write it to the list?

Click the Restore button.

Delete a record?

Display the record in the form, and click the Delete button.

Using AutoCorrect and AutoComplete

How do I...

Create an AutoCorrect entry?

Click Office Button → Excel Options, click the Proofing category header, and then click the AutoCorrect Options button. Enter the text you want to replace in the Replace field; enter the text to replace it in the With field (see Figure 2-5).

Figure 2-5. AutoCorrect entries correct common misspellings.

Undo an auto correction?

Press Ctrl-Z.

Control AutoCorrect options?

Click Office Button → Excel Options, click the Proofing category header, and then click the AutoCorrect Options button; select the checkboxes representing the types of changes you want Excel to make for you.

Turn off AutoCorrect?

Click Office Button → Excel Options, click the Proofing category header, and then click the AutoCorrect Options button; uncheck the "Replace text as you type" box.

Stop Excel from turning network paths into hyperlinks?

Click Office Button → Excel Options, click the Proofing category header, and then click the Auto-Correct Options button, click the AutoFormat As You Type tab and uncheck the "Internet and net-work paths with hyperlinks" box.

Let Excel finish entering a cell value for me?

If you type the first few characters of a value that exists in a cell directly above, Excel will offer to complete the current entry with that value. Press Enter to accept, or keep typing to finish the entry yourself.

Inserting Text and Other Elements

How do I...

Insert a symbol?

Click Insert → Symbol, then click the Symbols tab. Select the font and subset; click the symbol and click the Insert button. Click Cancel to close the Symbol dialog box.

Insert a special character?

Click Insert → Symbol → Special Characters; click the special character and click Insert.

Insert a page break?

Click Page Layout → Breaks → Insert Page Break. A horizontal page break appears in the row above the active cell. A vertical page break appears to the left of the column containing the active cell.

To insert only a horizontal break, select an entire row; to create only a vertical break, select an entire column.

Selecting Text and Data

How do I...

Select the entire contents of a cell?
    Click the cell.

Select multiple cells?
    Click the first cell you want to include, then drag the mouse pointer over the cells.

Select noncontiguous groups of cells?
    Select the first group of cells, then hold down the Ctrl key and select a second set of cells. Repeat with multiple groups.

Select data within a cell?
    Click the cell, and then highlight the cell contents in the Formula Bar, or double-click the cell and edit directly in the cell. (Make sure you previously clicked Office Button → Excel Options, clicked the Advance category header and then, in the "Editing options" group, checked the "Allow editing directly in cells" box.)

Cutting, Copying, and Pasting Data

How do I...

Cut data?
    Select the cell(s) you want to cut, and then click Home → Cut or press Ctrl-X.

Copy data?
    Select the cell(s) you want to copy, and then click Home → Copy or press Ctrl-C.

Paste data?
    Select the target cell(s), and then click Home → Paste or press Ctrl-V.

> **Paste data using Paste Special?**
>
> Select the target cell(s), click the Home tab, click the Paste button's down arrow, and click the desired paste operation. To see more options, click Paste Special to display the Paste Special dialog box. You can also right-click a cell or selection and click Paste Special from the shortcut menu that appears.

Display the Office Clipboard?

Click the Home tab, and then click the Clipboard group's dialog expander.

Paste an item from the Office Clipboard?

Click the Home tab, click the Clipboard group's dialog expander, and select the item in the clipboard list.

Paste every item from the Office Clipboard?

Click the Home tab, click the Clipboard group's dialog expander, and then click the Paste All button.

Remove an item from the Office Clipboard?

Click the Home tab, then click the Clipboard group's dialog expander; click the down arrow at the right edge of the item and select Delete.

Remove all items from the Office Clipboard?

Click the Home tab, click the Clipboard group's dialog expander, and click the Clear All button.

Change the behavior of the Office Clipboard?

Click the Home tab, click the Clipboard group's dialog expander, and then click the Options button.

Check the desired boxes, such as Show Office Clipboard Automatically.

Use the Paste Options button?

Click the Paste Options button and select the option button representing the formatting you want the pasted material to take on.

Hide the Paste Options button?
> Click Office Button → Excel Options, click the Advanced category header and then, in the "Cut, copy, and paste" section, uncheck the "Show Paste Options buttons" box.

Remove the marquee outline from around a copied group of cells?
> Press the Esc key.

Clearing Cell Contents and Formulas

How do I...

Clear cell data?
> Press the Delete key or click Home → Clear → Clear Contents.

Clear cell formatting?
> Click Home → Clear → Clear Formats.

Clear cell comments?
> Click Home → Clear → Clear Comments.

Clear all cell contents?
> Click Home → Clear → Clear All.

Formatting

Formatting Cell Contents

How do I...

Set the default font and font size?
> Click Office Button → Excel Options, click the Popular heading; using the controls in the When Creating New Workbooks section, choose the default font and size. You must close and restart Excel 2007 for the change to take effect.

Apply basic font formatting?

   Select the cells you want to format, click Home, and use the buttons in the Font group.

Format part of a cell's contents?

 Click the cell and, in the Formula bar, select the part of the contents you want to format. You can also double-click the cell and select the part you want to format directly. Use the buttons on the Home tab's Font group to format the cell contents.

Change the text color?

   Click the Font Color button to impose the current color. To change the color, click the down arrow on the button and select the color from the palette. The last color you picked appears as an underline on the button.

Change the orientation of the cell's contents?

   Click Home → Orientation. Either click a preset orientation or click Format Cell Alignment to display the Alignment tab of the Format Cells dialog box. In the Format Cells dialog box, type the number of degrees the text should be rotated, or drag the red pointer in the Orientation pane to the desired angle.

Align the contents of a cell?

   To set the vertical alignment, display the Home tab of the Ribbon and then, in the Alignment group, click the Top Align, Middle Align, or Bottom Align button. To set the horizontal alignment, click the Alignment group's Align Text Left, Center, or Align Text Right button.

   Applying some cell styles and formats can change a cell's horizontal alignment

Indent the contents of a cell?

   Display the Home → Increase Indent or Home → Decrease Indent. To set a custom indent, click the Home tab and then click the Alignment group's dialog box

---

expander to display the Format Cells dialog box's Alignment tab. In the Indent box, enter the number of characters you want to indent the entry.

Wrap text within a cell?
Display the Home → Wrap Text.

Shrink text to fit within the existing borders of the cell?
Click the Home tab of the Ribbon and then click the Alignment group's dialog box expander to display the Format Cells dialog box's Alignment tab. On the Alignment tab, click the "Shrink to fit" box.

Merge cells?
Select the cells you want to merge and then click Home → Merge and Center button. If you'd like to perform a different merge operation, click the "Merge and Center" button's down arrow and select the option you want to apply.

Split merged cells?
Select the merged cells.Then in the Home tab's Alignment group, click the "Merge and Center" button's down arrow and select Unmerge Cells.

Apply a style?
Click Home → Cell Styles, and select a style from the Style gallery (shown in Figure 2-6).

Add a style?
Format the contents of a cell and click Home → Cell Styles → New Cell Style. Type the name of your new style in the Style name box and click Add and OK.

Duplicate an existing style?
Click Home → Cell Styles; right-click the style you want to modify from the Style gallery and click Duplicate. Type a name for the new style and click OK.

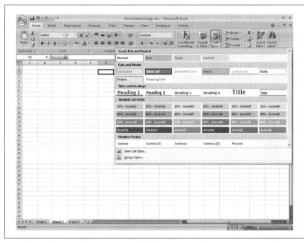

Figure 2-6. Clicking the Cell Styles button displays all of the styles available to you, plus links to tools for creating custom styles.

Modify a style?

Click Home → Cell Styles; right-click the style you want to modify from the Style gallery and click Modify. Use the controls in the Format Cells dialog box to change the style.

Delete a style?

Click Home → Cell Styles; right-click the style you want to modify from the Style gallery and click Delete.

Copy styles from another workbook?

Click Home → Cell Styles → Merge Styles and select the workbook that contains the styles you want.

Formatting Numbers and Dates

How do I...

Apply a preset format using a Ribbon button?

In the Home tab's Number group, click the Accounting Number Format, Percent Style, or Comma Style button to apply that format. If you want to apply another number format, click the Number Format list box's down arrow and select the format to apply.

Increase the number of decimal places?

Click Home → Increase Decimal button.

Decrease the number of decimal places?

Click Home → Decrease Decimal button.

Select a preset format?

On the Home tab of the Ribbon, click the Number group's dialog box expander to display the Format Cells dialog box. On the Number tab, click the category of format you want, and then click the specific format in the menus or lists to the right.

Create a custom format?

On the Home tab of the Ribbon, click the Number group's dialog box expander to display the Format Cells dialog box. On the Number tab, click Custom in the Category list. Click the format in the list to the right, and modify it in the Type box.

Create a conditional format?

Select the cells you want to format and then click Home → Conditional Formatting → Highlight Cells Rules. Click the type of conditional format you want to apply, and use the controls in the dialog box that appears to define your conditional format.

Conditionally format the top or bottom values in a list?

Select the cells you want to format and then click Home → Conditional Formatting → Top/Bottom Rules. Click the type of format you want to apply, and then use the controls in the dialog box that appears to specify the formatting and the number of values to be formatted.

Conditionally format above- or below-average values?

Select the cells you want to format, click Home → Conditional Formatting → Top/Bottom Rules, and then click either Above Average or Below Average. In the dialog box that appears, use the controls to specify the formatting to be applied.

TIP

The last item in the list of available formats is Custom Format, which lets you create your own format using the controls available in the Format Cells dialog box.

Summarize data conditionally using data bars?

Select the cells you want to format, click Home → Conditional Formatting → Data Bars, and then click the color data bar you want to apply.

Create a custom data bar conditional format?

Select the cells you want to format, click Home → Conditional Formatting → Data Bars → More Rules. Use the controls in the New Formatting Rule dialog box (shown in Figure 2-7) to determine whether to display just the data bar and not the cells' values, how to determine the length of the shortest and longest bar, and to select a color for the bar.

Summarize data conditionally using color scales?

Select the cells you want to format, click Home → Conditional Formatting → Color Scales, and then click the color scale you want to apply.

Create a custom color scale conditional format?

Select the cells you want to format, and click Home → Conditional Formatting → Color Scales → More Rules. Use the controls in the New Formatting Rule dialog box to select a 2- or 3-color scale, control how the conditional format changes the colors in the scale, and select the colors that make up the scale.

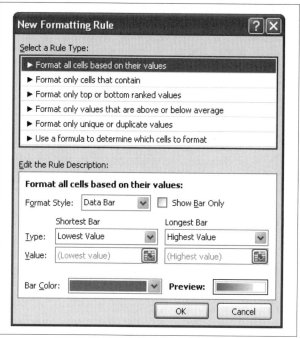

Figure 2-7. Customize your conditional format using the controls in the New Formatting Rule dialog box.

Summarize data conditionally using icon sets?

Select the cells you want to format, click Home → Conditional Formatting → Icon Sets, and then click the icon set you want to apply.

Create a custom icon set conditional format?

Select the cells you want to format, and click Home → Conditional Formatting → Icon Sets → More Rules. Use the controls in the New Formatting Rule dialog box to select an icon set, control how the conditional format selects which icon to display, whether to reverse the icons' order, and select whether to show the icon and not the cell value.

Reorder conditional formats?

Select the cells that contain the target conditional format and click Home → Conditional Formatting → Manage Rules. In the Conditional Formatting Rules Manager dialog box, click the rule you want to move and then click either the Move Up or Move Down button.

Edit conditional formats?

Select the cells that contain the target conditional format and click Home → Conditional Formatting → Manage Rules. In the Conditional Formatting Rules Manager dialog box, click the rule you want to edit and then click Edit Rule. Use the controls in the Edit Formatting Rule dialog box to make your changes.

Stop applying conditional formats after a condition is true?

Select the cells that contain the target conditional format and click Home → Conditional Formatting → Manage Rules. In the Conditional Formatting Rules Manager dialog box, check the Stop If True box next to any rule that, if its condition is true, should be the last rule to be followed.

Delete conditional formats?

Select the cells that contain the target conditional format and click Home → Conditional Formatting → Manage Rules. In the Conditional Formatting Rules Manager dialog box, click the rule you want to delete and then click Delete Rule.

Formatting Cell Borders and Areas

How do I...

Apply a border?

Select the cells, click the down arrow at the right edge of the Borders button in the Home tab's Font group, and select the pattern you want. You can also display the Home tab of the Ribbon, click the Font group's dialog box expander, click the Border tab, and pick the desired borders.

Draw borders around cells?

On the Home tab, in the Font group, click the down arrow at the right edge of the Borders button, and click Draw Border. When the mouse pointer changes to a pencil, use it to draw a border around a group of cells.

Hold down the Ctrl key and Excel will draw a full grid, not just a border around the cells. You can also click the right edge of the Borders button and click Draw Border Grid.

Erase existing borders?

Select the cells with borders you want to erase, click the down arrow at the right edge of the Borders button in the Home tab's Font group, and click No Borders. You can also click the Erase Border item on the same list and scrub away any cell borders.

Change the border's style?

Select the cells, click the down arrow at the right edge of the Borders button in the Home tab's Font group, click Line Style, and click the style you want.

Change the color of a border line?

Select the cells, click the down arrow at the right edge of the Borders button in the Home tab's Font group, click Line Color, and click the color you want.

Fill a cell with a color?

In the Home tab's Font group, click the Fill Color button's down arrow and select the desired color.

Fill a cell with a pattern?

On the Home tab of the Ribbon, click the Font group's dialog box expander to display the Format Cells dialog box. Click the Patterns tab. Open the Pattern Style menu and pick the pattern from the palette; then open the Pattern Color menu and pick the color from the palette.

Formatting a Workbook

How do I...

Apply an Office Theme?
> Click Page Layout → Themes, and then click the desired theme from the gallery that appears (Figure 2-8).

Modify an Office Theme?
> In the Page Layout tab's Themes group, use the Colors, Fonts, and Effects controls to select the settings you want to appear in your theme. Click Page Layout → Themes → Save Current Theme, and type a name for your new theme.

WARNING

Be sure to save your new theme in the default directory. If you don't, Office 2007 won't be able to find the theme or display it in the theme gallery.

Change the color of a sheet tab?
> Right-click the sheet tab, click Tab Color, and pick the color, or click Home → Format → Tab Color.

Working with Hyperlinks

The following answers show you how to create, remove, edit, and follow hyperlinks. You will also learn how to set a URL as a default value so you can just enter the page name (e.g., index2.htm) of a web page.

How do I...

Create a hyperlink?
> Click Insert → Hyperlink or Ctrl-K to display the Insert Hyperlink dialog box (Figure 2-9). Indicate the type of hyperlink using the buttons to the left ("Existing File or Web Page", "Place in This Document", or "E-mail Address") and fill in the fields. Click the "Browse for File" button to navigate and pick the file or location you want to link to.

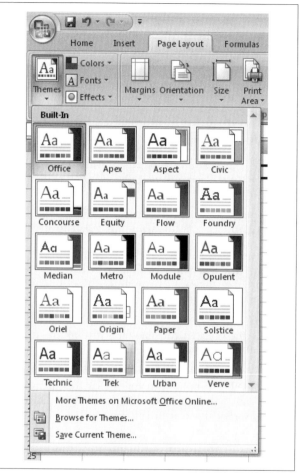

Figure 2-8. Select an existing Office Theme from the Themes gallery, or create one of your own.

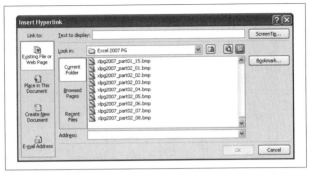

Figure 2-9. Use the Insert Hyperlink dialog box to create and edit your hyperlinks.

Remove a hyperlink?
> Right-click the cell and click Remove Hyperlink.

Edit a hyperlink?
> Right-click the cell, click Edit Hyperlink, and use the controls in the Edit Hyperlink dialog box to edit the hyperlink.

Follow a hyperlink?
> Click the cell that contains the hyperlink; Excel opens the address in a new browser window.

Set a hyperlink base that all hyperlinks in a workbook will use?
> Click Office Button → Properties, click the Summary tab, and enter a web address in the Hyperlink base field. You can override this base by entering a full URL (e.g., *http:// www.oreilly.com/*).

Working with Headers and Footers

Use these solutions to create headers and footers that will appear at the top and bottom of each printed page. You will learn how to add text, format it, add changing values (such as the current time or page number), and add images.

How do I...

View a workbook in Page Layout View?
Click View → Page Layout.

Create a header or footer with AutoText?
Click Insert → Header and Footer. In the Design contextual tab's Header & Footer group, click either the Header or Footer button and select the AutoText you want to fill the header or footer.

Add custom text to a header or footer?
Click Insert → Header and Footer. If necessary, in the Design contextual tab's Navigation group, click either the "Go to Header" or "Go to Footer" button to activate the header or footer. Click the left, center, or right section of the header or footer, and type text in the section.

Format text in a custom header or footer?
Select the text, click Home, and use the controls in the Font group to format the text.

Add the printed page number to a header or footer?
Click Insert → Header and Footer, and then click the header or footer section where you want the page number to appear. In the Design contextual tab's Header & Footer Elements group, click the Page Number button (Figure 2-10).

Figure 2-10. Use the controls on the Header & Footer Tools Design contextual tab to define the contents of your header and footer.

Print the total number of pages in a worksheet as a header or footer?

Click Insert → Header and Footer, then click the header or footer section where you want the number of pages to appear. In the Design contextual tab's Header & Footer Elements group, click the "Number of Pages" button.

Include the current time in a header or footer?

Click Insert → Header and Footer, and then click the header or footer section where you want the time to appear. In the Design contextual tab's Header & Footer Elements group, click the Current Time button.

Include the current date in a header or footer?

Click Insert → Header and Footer, and then click the header or footer section where you want the date to appear. In the Design contextual tab's Header & Footer Elements group, click the Current Date button.

Include the workbook's file and path information in a custom header or footer?

Click Insert → Header and Footer, and then click the header or footer section where you want the file and path information to appear. In the Design contextual tab's Header & Footer Elements group, click the File Path button.

Include the file name of the active workbook in a custom header or footer?

Click Insert → Header and Footer, and then click the header or footer section where you want the file name to appear. In the Design contextual tab's Header & Footer Elements group, click the File Name button.

Include the worksheet's name in a custom header or footer?

Click Insert → Header and Footer, and then click the header or footer section where you want the sheet name to appear. In the Design contextual tab's Header & Footer Elements group, click the Sheet Name button.

Edit a picture in a custom header or footer?

Click Insert → Header and Footer, and then click the header or footer section that contains the picture. Then, in the Design contextual tab's Header & Footer Elements group, click the Format Picture button. Use the controls in the Format Picture dialog box to change the picture's appearance.

Change the margins of a header or footer?

On the Page Layout tab, click the Page Setup group's dialog expander. In the Page Setup dialog box, click the Margins tab. Type the new margins in the Header and Footer boxes.

Summarizing Data

The following answers show you how to display running totals for selected data, add formulas to cells, edit formulas, identify formula precedents and dependents, check formulas for errors, and watch how the values in selected cells change as other worksheet data changes.

Getting a Running Total

How do I...

Display a running total on the status bar?

Select the cells. The sum, average, and count of the selected cells appear at the bottom right of the screen in the status bar.

Change how selected cells are calculated on the status bar?

Right-click the status bar, and click the names of the operations you want to add to or clear from the status bar. Unlike in previous versions of Excel, you can display all six available summaries (sum, count, numerical count, average, minimum, and maximum) on the status bar at once.

Adding Formulas to Cells

How do I...

Type a formula into a cell?

Type = and then enter the rest of the formula.

Add a function to a formula using Formula AutoComplete?

Type = and then type the first letter or letters of the function. Click the desired function from the Formula Auto-Complete list and press Tab to add it to the formula.

Edit a formula in a cell?

Click the cell and edit the formula on the formula bar. You can also double-click the cell and edit directly.

Create a summation formula quickly?

Select a cell below the cells you want to sum and click Formulas → AutoSum to create the formula. Verify the range.

Create other kinds of formulas quickly?

Select a cell below the cells you want to sum and click the down arrow at the bottom of the AutoSum button. Select the function you want from the list, or click More Functions to select any available function using the Insert Function dialog box.

NOTE

Press Esc to abort entering a formula into a cell.

Add a formula using the Insert Function dialog box?

Click Formulas → Insert Function.

Turn off formula help ScreenTips?

Click Office Button → Excel Options, click the Advanced header and then, in the Display section, uncheck the "Show function ScreenTips" box.

Show or hide the formula bar?

Click Office Button → Excel Options, click the Advanced tab and then, in the Display section, uncheck the "Show formula bar" box.

Create formulas with relative references?

Type the cell references without dollar signs, such as in the formula =SUM(C6:C9). When you create a formula with relative references, Excel will change the cells used in the formula to reflect the formula's new location. For example, if you typed the formula =SUM(C6:C9) in cell A1 and copied the formula to cell B2, which is one row below and one column to the right of its original position, Excel would change the formula to =SUM(D7:D10).

Create formulas with absolute references?

Type the cell references in a formula with dollar signs in front of the column letter and row number, such as in the formula =SUM($C$6:$C$9). If you typed this formula into cell A1 and copied it to cell B2, the formula would stay exactly the same.

Change between absolute and relative references?

To change an individual cell reference between absolute and relative references, click the cell that contains the formula and then, on the formula bar, select the reference you want to change and press F4. Pressing F4 once changes the reference to absolute rows and columns, pressing it twice results in relative columns and absolute rows, pressing it a third time results in absolute columns and relative rows, and pressing it a fourth time results in relative columns and relative rows.

Auditing Formulas

How do I...

Trace a cell's precedents?

Click Formulas → Trace Precedents.

Trace a cell's dependents?

Click Formulas → Trace Dependents.

Remove precedent arrows?

On the Formulas tab, click the Remove Arrows button's down arrow, and then click Remove Precedent Arrows.

Remove dependent arrows?

On the Formulas tab, click the Remove Arrows button's down arrow, and then click Remove Dependent Arrows.

Remove all arrows?

Click Formulas → Remove Arrows.

Trace the source of an error?

On the Formulas tab, click the Error Checking button's down arrow, and then click Trace Errors.

Circle invalid data?

In the Data tab's Data Tools group, click the Data Validation button's down arrow, and then click Circle Invalid Data.

Clear validation circles?

In the Data tab's Data Tools group, click the Data Validation button's down arrow, and then click Clear Validation Circles.

Show the Watch Window?

Click Formulas → Watch Window.

Add a watch?

Click Formulas → Watch Window, click the Add Watch button; select the cell(s) to watch and click the Add button.

Delete a watch?

Click Formulas → Watch Window; click the watch and click the Delete Watch button.

Evaluate a formula?

Select the cell that contains the formula. Click Formulas → Evaluate Formula. Click the Evaluate button. To perform the next calculation in a formula, click the Step In button. To move to the result of the previous calculation in the formula, click the Step Out button.

Using Named Ranges

The following answers show you how to streamline cell references by creating, renaming, editing, and deleting named ranges, as well as demonstrating how to use named ranges in formulas.

How do I...

Create a named range?

Select the cells you want in the range and click Formulas → Define Name. Type the name of the range in the Name field and click OK.

Use a named range in a formula?

Type the name of the range in the formula where you would normally put the names of the cells, such as =SUM(Week1) instead of =SUM(A7:A13). The available named ranges appear in the Formula AutoComplete list as you type the formula.

Delete a named range?

Click Formulas → Name Manager. Select the range, click the Delete button, and click OK to verify the operation.

Rename a named range?

Click Formulas → Name Manager. Select the range and click Edit. Type a new name for the range and click OK.

Change the cells in a named range?

Click Formulas → Name Manager. Select the range. Select the text in the "Refers to" field, click the button on the right end of the field, select the new group of cells, click the button again, then click OK.

Defining Alternative Data Sets

The following answers show you how to extend the usability of a worksheet by defining alternative data sets, called scenarios. You will learn how to create, display, and edit scenarios; bring in scenarios from other workbooks; and summarize scenarios on a new worksheet.

How do I...

Create a scenario?

Click Data → What-If Analysis → Scenario Manager, click the Add button. Type a name in the "Scenario name" field. Click in the "Changing cells" field, click the button on the right end of the field, select the cells you want to change, click the button again, then click OK. In the Scenario Values dialog box, type the new values for the listed cells and click OK.

NOTE

You can change up to 32 cells in a scenario.

Display a scenario?

Click Data → What-If Analysis → Scenario Manager. Click the scenario you want to display and click the Show button.

NOTE

If you close a workbook with a scenario displayed, those values are saved as the new values for the changed cells. It is a good idea to create a "normal" scenario that contains the original values in your worksheet so you can restore them if you close your workbook while a scenario is displayed.

Edit a scenario?

Click Data → What-If Analysis → Scenario Manager. Select the scenario and click the Edit button. Type a new name in the "Scenario name" field. Click in the "Changing cells" field, select the cells you want to change, and click OK. In the Scenario Values dialog box, enter new values for the listed cells and click OK.

Merge scenarios from another worksheet?

Click Data → What-If Analysis → Scenario Manager, click the Merge button. In the Merge Scenarios dialog box, open the Book menu, select the desired workbook, and click OK.

Summarize existing scenarios?

Click Data → What-If Analysis → Scenario Manager, click the Summary button. Save the summary as a standard report or PivotTable, click in the Results cells field, select the cells containing the formulas that change as a result of the changed scenario data, and click OK.

Delete a scenario?

Click Data → What-If Analysis → Scenario Manager. Select the scenario and click the Delete button.

Find the value needed in one cell to produce a given result from a formula?

Click Data → What-If Analysis → Goal Seek. Type the name (or address) of the cell with the result you want to change, enter the target value for that cell, and select the cell to vary to achieve that result.

Controlling How Data Is Displayed

Use the following solutions to change the order of the data in your worksheets; limit what data is displayed; have Excel calculate subtotals for groups of data; and to define views that incorporate filter, sorting, and hidden row/column settings.

Sorting Worksheet Data

How do I...

Sort a column in ascending order?

Click a cell in the column, then click Home → Sort & Filter → Sort A to Z.

Sort a column in descending order?

Click a cell in the column, then click Home → Sort & Filter → Sort Z to A.

Make a sort case-sensitive?

Click Home → Sort & Filter → Custom Sort. Click the sorting rule you want to make case sensitive, and click Options. Check the "Case sensitive" box.

Sort a subset of a column's values?

Select the cells to sort, and select the desired sorting option. If the Sort Warning dialog appears, select "Continue with the current selection" and click Sort.

Sort multiple columns by the values in the left-most column?

Select the cells to sort and select the desired sorting option.

Sort multiple columns based on a user-defined order?

Select the cells to sort and click Home → Sort & Filter → Custom Sort. Define the primary sorting criteria in the Sort By section; you can add more criteria by clicking Add Level and filling in the Then By sections.

Create custom data lists?

Type a list of values in a column, click Office Button → Excel Options, click the Popular category heading, and then click the Edit Custom Lists button. In the Custom Lists dialog box, verify that the cells appear in the "Import list from cells" field and click the Import button.

Sort using a custom data list?

Select the cells to sort, click Home → Sort & Filter → Custom Sort, click the Order down arrow, click Custom List, and then, in the Custom Lists dialog box, click the custom list by which you want to sort the data.

Sort by cell color?

Select the cells to sort, click Home → Sort & Filter → Custom Sort, click the Sort On down arrow, and click Cell Color. Click the Order down arrow, click the color you want to appear at the top or bottom of the sorted list, and then select either On Top or On Bottom from the final list box in the criteria row.

Sort by font color?

Select the cells to sort, click Home → Sort & Filter → Custom Sort, click the Sort On down arrow, and click Font Color. Click the Order down arrow, click the color you want to appear at the top or bottom of the sorted list, and then select either On Top or On Bottom from the final list box in the criteria row.

Sort by cell icon?

Select the cells to sort, click Home → Sort & Filter → Custom Sort, click the Sort On down arrow, and click Cell Icon. Click the Order down arrow, click the icon you want to appear at the top or bottom of the sorted list, and then select either On Top or On Bottom from the final list box in the criteria row.

Filtering Worksheet Data

How do I...

Create an AutoFilter?

Click a cell in the data to filter and click Home → Sort & Filter → Filter. Click the down arrow that appears in the header row of your data and select the desired filter.

Remove an AutoFilter?
Click Home → Sort & Filter and uncheck Filter.

Display the top or bottom n values in a column that contains numerical data?
Click Home → Sort & Filter → Filter. Click the down arrow of a column, click Number Filters, and click Top 10. From the menus, select Top or Bottom. Set the number of values to display by specifying the number of Items, or by specifying a Percent of total items.

Display all values in a column?
Click Home → Sort & Filter → Filter. Click the down arrow in the first cell of the column and select (All).

Create a custom AutoFilter?
Click the down arrow in the first cell of the column, point to Number Filter (or Text Filter or Date Filter), and click Custom Filter. Specify the criteria for filtering the selected cells.

NOTE

The relevant menu item changes to reflect the type of data in the column. If the data is of mixed types (that is, some text, some numbers, and some dates), the menu item will be Number Filter.

Create an advanced filter?
Type the headings of the list you want to filter and the filter criteria in cells in the worksheet that contains the data to be filtered (Figure 2-11). In the Data tab's Sort & Filter group, click Advanced. In the List Range field, select the cells to be filtered. In the Criteria Range field, select the cells that contain the criteria, and click OK.

Copy the results of an advanced filter to another location?
Create an advanced filter and select "Copy to another location." In the Copy To field, select the cell at the top-left corner of the range where you want to copy the filtered data, and click OK.

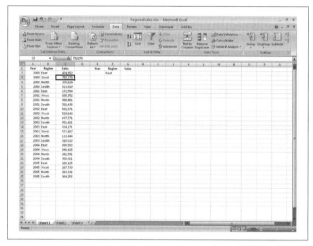

Figure 2-11. Copy the headers from your data list and fill in the filter's expressions to create an Advanced Filter in Excel 2007.

Find unique rows only?

Create an advanced filter and check the Unique Records Only box.

Using Subtotals to Summarize Data

How do I...

Add subtotals to a worksheet?

Create a data list. The list must have labeled columns and any column you want subtotals for must be sorted. Click Data → Subtotal. Select the column to be subtotaled, select the function (e.g., sum), and whether the summary should be below the data.

Add a detail level?

In a data list with existing subtotals, select the rows you want to define as a new detail level, and click Data → Group.

Remove a detail level?

In a data list with existing subtotals, select the rows you want to remove as a detail level, and click Data → Ungroup.

Hide a detail level?

Click the Hide Detail button (the button to the left with a minus sign) at the bottom of the rows in that level.

Display a detail level?

Click the Show Detail button (the button to the left with a plus sign) next to a group of hidden rows.

Creating Custom Views

How do I...

Add a custom view?

Apply filters, print settings, and hidden rows and columns to your worksheet. Click View → Custom Views and click the Add button. Supply a name for the view, and check the boxes indicating which elements (such as print settings) you want to include in the view.

Display a custom view?

Click View → Custom Views; select the view and click the Display button.

Delete a custom view?

Click View → Custom Views; select the view and click the Delete button.

Protecting All or Part of a Workbook

How do I...

Protect a worksheet?

Click Review → Protect Sheet. In the dialog box, type a password users can enter to remove the protection, and check the boxes for every action users are allowed to perform in this workbook.

Unprotect the worksheet if it's protected, select the range to be protected, and then Review → Allow Users to Edit Ranges. Click the New button, type a title for the range and a password to unlock it and confirm the password, and click OK. Now protect the worksheet using the steps in the previous item.

Protect a workbook?

Click Review → Protect Workbook. Type a password that must be entered to access the workbook.

Protect and share a workbook?

Click Review → Protect and Share Workbook. Check the "Sharing with track changes" box, and type a password that must be entered to access the workbook.

Spelling and Other Tools

Use the following answers to find and correct misspelled words, to create custom dictionaries, and to select which types of cell values you want to check.

How do I...

Perform a spellcheck on a worksheet?

Click Review → Spelling or press F7. The Spelling dialog box (Figure 2-12) flags errors and suggests replacements.

1. **Not in Dictionary.** This box displays the term the Spelling Checker can't find in its dictionaries. You can type a word or phrase in this box, and click Change to replace the questioned term with the word or phrase you typed.

2. **Suggestions.** This box displays a list of words or phrases that Excel determines to be likely replacements for the questioned text. You can apply a suggestion by clicking it and clicking Change.

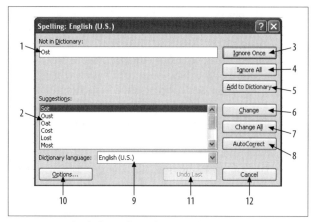

Figure 2-12. Check the spelling of your worksheet. You can choose which elements to check so Excel doesn't get hung up on errors that aren't errors.

3. **Ignore Once.** Clicking Ignore Once causes the Spelling Checker to pass by the error displayed in the "Not in Dictionary" box without correcting it. The Spelling Checker will identify the same text as an error if it occurs again within the worksheet, and it will identify the same instance as an error the next time you check the worksheet's spelling.

4. **Ignore All.** Clicking Ignore All causes the Spelling Checker to pass by every instance of the error displayed in the "Not in Dictionary" box (not just the highlighted error) without correcting it. The Spelling Checker will identify the same text as an error the next time you check the worksheet's spelling.

5. **Add to Dictionary.** Clicking "Add to Dictionary" adds the questioned term into the active custom dictionary.

6. **Change.** Clicking Change replaces the questioned term with the highlighted word or phrase displayed in the Suggestions box.

7. **Change All.** Clicking Change All replaces every instance of the questioned term with the highlighted word or phrase displayed in the Suggestions box.

8. **AutoCorrect.** Clicking AutoCorrect creates an AutoCorrect rule where the questioned term is automatically replaced by the word or phrase displayed in the Suggestions box.

9. **Dictionary Language.** Clicking the Dictionary Language down arrow lets you select a new dictionary to use in the spelling check. Alternative dictionaries include English (British), French, and Spanish.

10. **Options.** Clicking Options displays the Spelling Options dialog box, where you can decide which elements in your worksheet, such as hyperlinks or numbers, should be checked for spelling errors.

11. **Undo Last.** Clicking Undo Last negates the last change and displays the previous misspelling.

12. **Cancel.** Clicking Cancel closes the Spelling dialog box without taking any further actions.

Spell check words with numbers, that are all uppercase, or that are Internet or file addresses?

Click Review → Spelling, click the Options button. Uncheck the "Ignore words with numbers," "Ignore words in UPPERCASE," and "Ignore Internet and file address" checkboxes.

Add words to the current custom dictionary?

Click Review → Spelling, display the word you want to add, and then click Add to Dictionary.

Create a new custom dictionary?
> Click Review → Spelling. Click the Options button and then, in the Excel Options dialog box, click the Custom Dictionaries button. Click New, type a name for the new custom dictionary, and click Save.

Change the default custom dictionary?
> Click Review → Spelling. Click the Options button and then, in the Excel Options dialog box, click the Custom Dictionaries button. Click the dictionary you want to make the default custom dictionary, and click Change Default.

Edit the contents of a custom dictionary?
> Click Review → Spelling. Click the Options button and then, in the Excel Options dialog box, click the Custom Dictionaries button. Click the dictionary you want to edit and then click Edit Word List. In the dialog box that appears, use the controls to add new entries and modify existing entries.

Customizing Excel

The answers in this section show you how to change the Excel user interface, control whether Excel displays a preview of formatting changes before you make the change, add and remove buttons from the Quick Access Toolbar, and control where the Quick Access Toolbar appears.

Setting General Customization Options

Excel 2007 offers several new customization options, most of which reflect new program capabilities. Live Preview, for example, displays the results of a formatting change when you hover the mouse pointer over a button that would change an object within your workbook. The Mini Toolbar, which is an elaboration of the shortcut menu, appears when you select an object and offers the most popular controls (e.g., the Bold toolbar button) for your use. If you want to create macros, you can display the Developer tab to gain access to those tools. Finally, if you want to turn off the Screen Tips that appear when you hover the mouse pointer over a workbook object, you can do so.

How do I...

Enable Live Preview?
Click Office Button → Excel Options, click the Popular category heading and then, in the "Top options for working with Excel" section, check the Enable Live Preview box. To disable Live Preview, uncheck the box.

Display the Mini Toolbar when selecting cells or worksheet objects?
Click Office Button → Excel Options, click the Popular category heading and then, in the "Top options for working with Excel" section, check the "Show Mini Toolbar on selection" box. To disable the Mini Toolbar, uncheck the box.

Show the Developer tab?
Click Office Button → Excel Options, click the Popular category heading and then, in the "Top options for working with Excel" section, check the "Show Developer tab in the Ribbon" box. To hide the Developer tab, uncheck the box.

Select a color scheme?
Click Office Button → Excel Options, click the Popular category heading and then, in the "Top options for working with Excel" section, click the "Color scheme" box's down arrow and select the desired color scheme.

Show or hide ScreenTips?
Click Office Button → Excel Options, click the Popular category heading and then, in the "Top options for working with Excel" section, click the "ScreenTip style" box's down arrow and select the desired way to display Screen Tips.

Customizing the Quick Access Toolbar

How do I...

Add a button to the Quick Access Toolbar?
Click Office Button → Excel Options, click the Customize category heading, and select the command you want to add. Click the Add button.

Change the order of buttons on the Quick Access Toolbar?
Click Office Button → Excel Options, and click the Customize category heading. In the righthand command list, which represents the commands on the Quick Access Toolbar, click the button you want to move and then click either the Move Up or Move Down button.

Remove a button from the Quick Access Toolbar?
Right-click the button and click "Remove from Quick Access Toolbar".

Move the Quick Access Toolbar below the Ribbon?
Right-click any item on the Quick Access Toolbar and click "Show Quick Access Toolbar Below the Ribbon".

NOTE

Moving the Quick Access Toolbar below the Ribbon gives you a lot more space to add buttons.

Hide or show the Ribbon?
Press Ctrl-F1 or right-click any item on the Ribbon or the Quick Access Toolbar and click "Minimize the Ribbon". To restore the Ribbon, press Ctrl-F1 again or right-click any of the Ribbon tabs that are still displayed.

Collaborating

Use these answers to add, delete, and edit worksheet comments; to control how comments are displayed; to track workbook changes; and to accept or reject any or all of those changes.

Comments

How do I...

Insert a comment?
> Click Review → New Comment or press Shift-F2.

Edit a comment?
> Click the cell that contains the comment and click Review → Edit Comment (or right-click the comment and click Edit Comment).

Delete a comment?
> Click the cell that contains the comment and click Review → Delete (or right-click the comment and click Delete Comment).

Display a comment?
> Place the pointer over the cell.

Display the next comment?
> Click Review → Next.

Display the previous comment?
> Click Review → Previous.

Show or hide a specific comment?
> Click Review → Show/Hide Comment.

Display all comments?
> Click Review → Show All Comments. The button changes to indicate it has been selected. Click it to hide all comments.

Tracking Changes

How do I...

Turn on change tracking?

Click Review → Track Changes → Highlight Changes
and check the "Track changes while editing" box.

Specify which changes to track?

Click Review → Track Changes → Highlight Changes
and check the "Track changes while editing" box. Check
the When, Who, and Where boxes to track changes
based on when they were made, which user made them,
and in which part of the workbook the changes were
made. Use items on each box's down list to select which
specific changes to track.

Display or hide all changes?

Click Review → Track Changes → Highlight Changes
and check the "Track changes while editing" box. Check
or uncheck "Highlight changes on screen" (Figure 2-13).

Prevent changes from being removed?

Click Review → Protect Shared Workbook. In the Protect Shared Workbook dialog box, check the "Sharing
with track changes" box, and type a password that must
be entered to access the workbook.

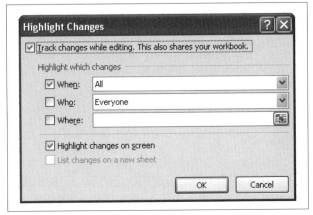

*Figure 2-13. Limit which changes you track by setting rules in the
Highlight Changes dialog box.*

Accept a change?

Click Review → Track Changes → Accept/Reject
Changes, pick the changes and click OK, then click the
Accept button.

Accept all changes?

Click Review → Track Changes → Accept/Reject
Changes, pick the changes and click OK, then click the
Accept All button.

Reject a change?

Click Review → Track Changes → Accept/Reject
Changes, pick the changes and click OK, then click the
Reject button.

Reject all changes in a worksheet?

Click Review → Track Changes → Accept/Reject
Changes, pick the changes and click OK, then click the
Reject All button.

Track changes on a separate worksheet?
　　Click Review → Track Changes → Highlight Changes,
　　check the "Track changes while editing" box. Check the
　　"List changes on a new sheet" box.

Sharing Workbooks

How do I...

Allow changes by more than one user at a time?
　　Click Review → Share Workbook. Check the "Allow
　　changes by more than one user at the same time" box.

Determine how long to keep a change history?
　　Click Review → Share Workbook. On the Advanced tab,
　　select the "Keep change history for" option and enter the
　　number of days to keep the change history in the
　　option's spin box.

Specify when to update changes?
　　Click Review → Share Workbook. On the Advanced tab,
　　in the "Update changes" section, select the "When file is
　　saved" option to save all changes when anyone saves the
　　file, or select the "Automatically every" option to deter-
　　mine how often to update the changes. You can also
　　choose whether to save your changes and see other users'
　　changes, or to have Excel display the other users'
　　changes only.

Determine which changes have precedence?
　　Click Review → Share Workbook. On the Advanced tab,
　　in the "Conflicting changes between users" section,
　　select the "Ask me which changes win" option to list
　　each changed cell with the changes offered for that cell,
　　or select "The changes being saved win" to always have
　　the most recent change take precedence.

Specify which items to include in your personal view?
Click Review → Share Workbook. On the Advanced tab, in the "Include in personal view" section, check the "Print settings" or "Filter settings" box to include those items in your personal view of the shared workbook.

Working with the Web

The answers in this section show you how to save a worksheet or workbook as a web document, and how to update web documents based on a workbook.

How do I...

Save a worksheet as a web page?
Click Office Button → Save As → Other Formats. In the Save As dialog box, click the "Save as type" down arrow and select Web Page (*.htm; *.html), and then click "Selection: Sheet."

Save a workbook as a web page?
Click Office Button → Save As → Other Formats. In the Save As dialog box, click the "Save as type" down arrow and select Web Page (*.htm; *.html), and then click Entire Workbook.

Change the title of an Excel web page?
Click Office Button → Save As → Other Formats. In the Save As dialog box, click the Change Title button, enter a new title, and click OK.

Publish a page to the Web?

Click Office Button → Save As → Other Formats. In the Save As dialog box, click the "Save as type" down arrow and select Web Page (*.htm; *.html), and then click the Publish button. In the "Publish as Web Page" dialog box, click the Publish button.

Update the published page every time the source workbook is saved?

    Click Office Button → Save As → Other Formats. In the Save As dialog box, click the "Save as type" down arrow and select Web Page (*.htm; *.html), click the Publish button, and check the "AutoRepublish every time this workbook is saved" box. Click the Publish button.

Open the published web page in a browser when you publish it?

    Click Office Button → Save As → Other Formats. In the Save As dialog box, click the "Save as type" down arrow and select Web Page (*.htm; *.html), click the Publish button, and check the "Open Published Web Page in Browser" box. Click the Publish button.

Summarizing Data with Charts

The solutions in this section show you how to represent worksheet data in charts, to change a chart's formatting or type, and to add a trend line to a chart that displays a series of data.

How do I...

Insert a chart?

    In the Insert tab's Charts group, click the type of chart you want to create (e.g., Column), and then click the desired chart subtype.

Change a chart type?

    Click the chart and, if necessary, click the Design contextual tab. Click the Change Chart Type button and select the new type.

Remove a chart's data series?

    Click the chart and, if necessary, click the Design contextual tab. Click the Select Data button, click the data series, and click Remove.

Add a data series to a chart?

Click the chart and, if necessary, click the Design contextual tab. Click the Select Data button and click Add. In the Edit Series dialog box, type a name for the new data series in the "Series name" field, click in the "Series values" field, and select the values you want to add to the chart.

Edit a data series?

Click the chart and, if necessary, click the Design contextual tab. Click the Select Data button, select the series you want to edit, and click Edit. In the Edit Series dialog box, make the desired changes.

TIP

If you create a chart that contains only numerical series, such as years in one column and total sales in the other, Excel will display both sets of values in the main body of the chart and use a generic series (i.e., 1, 2, 3...) for the horizontal axis values. To use one data series as the values for the horizontal axis, delete the series from the Legend Entries (Series) list and edit the Horizontal (Category) Axis Labels data series so it refers to the values you want displayed on that axis.

Change the format of a chart element?

Right-click the chart element (such as the legend) and click the last item on the shortcut menu, which starts with "Format" and is followed by the name of the element (e.g., Format Chart Area, Format Legend, and so on). Use the controls in the dialog box to modify the element's appearance.

Change the layout of a chart?

Click the chart and, if necessary, click the Design contextual tab. Select the desired layout from the Chart Layouts gallery.

Change a chart's color scheme?

Click the chart and, if necessary, click the Design contextual tab. Click the Chart Styles group's More button and select the desired color scheme from the gallery.

Add chart labels?

Click the chart and, if necessary, click the Layout contextual tab. Click the Labels group's Data Labels button and select the type of labels you want to display on the chart.

Add a trend line to a chart?

Click the chart and then click the Analysis group's Trendline button. From the options that appear, click Linear.

Add a forward-looking trend line to a chart?

Click the chart and then click the Analysis group's Trendline button. From the options that appear, click More Trendline Options. Click the Trendline Options category header and, in the Forecast section, type the number of periods you want to extend the trend line (if any), and click OK.

Move a chart to its own sheet?

Click the chart and, if necessary, click the Design contextual tab. Click the Move Chart button and select a new location for the chart.

Analyzing Data with PivotTables and PivotCharts

The answers in this section show you how to create, edit, and use PivotTables and PivotCharts—a handy way to create a dynamic summary of Excel or database information. You will also learn how to format PivotTables and PivotCharts, and how to filter data displayed in PivotTables and PivotCharts.

How do I...

Prepare data for use in a PivotTable or PivotChart?

To begin, your data must be arranged as a list, as shown in Figure 2-14. The list must have column headings, and there can't be any stray values in adjoining columns. The easiest way to create such a list in Excel 2007 is to create an Excel table by clicking any cell in the data list, clicking Home → Format as Table, and clicking the desired table format.

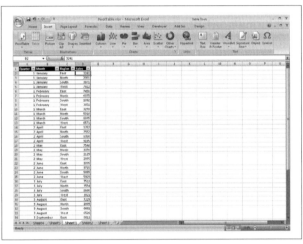

Figure 2-14. Your data must be in list format, with column headings, so Excel can turn it into a PivotTable.

Create a PivotTable?

Click a cell in your data list and click Insert → Pivot-Table. In the Create PivotTable dialog box, verify that the correct data source appears in the Table/Range field and that the New Worksheet option is selected. Click OK to create a PivotTable that contains each of the data source's columns as potential fields. In the "Choose fields to add to report" section of the PivotTable Field

List task pane, drag the appropriate fields to the Column Labels and Row Labels areas, drag fields you'll use to filter your data to the Report Filter area, and drag fields with data that will populate the PivotTable to the Values area.

Pivot a PivotTable?

Drag the field header to the desired position in the Pivot-Table layout. A gray bar will indicate where the field will be placed.

Edit PivotTable data?

On the worksheet with the list used to create the Pivot-Table, type in the new values. Click the PivotTable and click Options → Refresh Data.

Add data to a PivotTable without using an Excel table?

Add new rows of data to the data list and note the number of the last row that now contains data. Click the PivotTable, click the Options contextual tab, and click Change Data Source. In the Table/Range field, edit the range it contains to reflect the rows of data you added. Click Options → Refresh.

Add data to a PivotTable created using data in an Excel table?

Add new rows of data to the Excel table, click the Pivot-Table, and then click Options → Refresh.

Apply PivotTable style to a PivotTable?

 Click the PivotTable and then, on the Design contextual tab, click the desired style from the Pivot-Table Styles gallery.

Filter a PivotTable?

Click the down arrow at the right edge of any field header. Check the boxes of the values you want to display, or uncheck boxes next to the values you want to hide. Click OK.

Link to data in a PivotTable?

Type = in the active cell of the source worksheet, go to the worksheet with the PivotTable, and click the cell in the PivotTable that contains the data you want to link to. Excel creates a formula for you.

Create a PivotChart?

Click a cell in your data list and then, on the Insert tab of the Ribbon, click the PivotTable button's down arrow and select PivotChart. In the Create PivotTable with PivotChart dialog box, verify that the correct data source appears in the Table/Range field and that the New Worksheet option is selected. Click OK to create a Pivot-Table that contains each of the data source's columns as potential fields. In the "Choose fields to add to report" section of the PivotTable Field List task pane, drag the appropriate fields to the Legend Fields and Axis Fields areas, drag fields you'll use to filter your data to the Report Filter area, and drag fields with data that will populate the PivotTable to the Values area.

Pivot a PivotChart?

In the PivotTable associated with the PivotChart, drag the field header to the desired position in the PivotTable layout. A gray bar indicates where the field will be placed.

Edit PivotChart data?

On the worksheet with the list used to create the Pivot-Table, type in the new values. Click the PivotTable and click Options → Refresh Data.

Filter a PivotChart?

In the PivotChart Filter Pane, click the down arrow next to the name of the field by which you want to filter your PivotChart and check the boxes of the values you want to display, or uncheck the boxes next to the values you want to hide.

CHAPTER 3

Formula Reference

This chapter provides quick but detailed references to the most useful functions in Excel 2007. You probably already use some of these functions, but you'll probably encounter a few that you haven't used before. You'll find the following sections in this chapter:

- New formulas in Excel 2007
- Math formulas
- Date and time formulas
- Financial formulas
- Lookup and reference formulas
- Logical formulas
- Text formulas
- Statistical formulas

New Formulas in Excel 2007

In response to user requests, the Excel product team created six new worksheet functions:

AVERAGEIF
    Calculates the average of cells that meet a single criteria.

AVERAGEIFS
    Calculates the average of cells that meet multiple criteria.

SUMIFS

Finds the sum of cells that meet multiple criteria (the SUMIF function, which calculates the sum of cells that meet a single criteria, was present in earlier versions of Excel).

COUNTIFS

Counts the number of cells that meet multiple criteria (the COUNTIF function, which counts the number of cells that meet a single criteria, was present in earlier versions of Excel).

RANDBETWEEN

Returns a random integer between two values you define.

IFERROR

Displays a custom message if a cell contains an error.

You find detailed descriptions of each of these new functions later in this section.

NOTE

In Excel 2003 and earlier, you had to install the Analysis ToolPak to use many advanced statistical functions. Those functions, which include chi-squared distribution and ANOVA analysis tools, are built into Excel 2007.

Math Formulas

Use the following functions to perform mathematical calculations on your worksheet data.

COMBIN

 COMBIN(number, number_chosen)

The COMBIN function finds the number of possible combinations when you select *number_chosen* items from a collection that is *number* in size. When you calculate the number of possible combinations, you don't care in which order the items are selected (e.g., 1, 2, 3 is the same as 3, 2, 1 and 2, 1, 3). If the order of the selected items does matter, you should use the PERMUT function to calculate the number of possible permutations.

Example: =COMBIN(52, 5) returns 2,598,960.

FACT

FACT(number)

The FACT function finds the factorial of a *number*, which is defined as multiplying each counting number from 1 to number (e.g., the factorial of 4 is 1 * 2 * 3 * 4, or 24).

Example: =FACT(8) returns 40,320.

INT

INT(number)

The INT function returns the integer component of a *number* by removing (truncating) any decimal part of *number*.

Example: =INT(14.7) returns 14.

PERMUT

PERMUT(number, number_chosen)

The PERMUT function finds the number of possible permutations when you select *number_chosen* items from a collection that is *number* in size. When you calculate the number of possible permutations, you do care in which order the items are selected (e.g., 1, 2, 3 is different than 2, 3, 1). If the order of the selected items doesn't matter, you should use the COMBIN function to calculate the number of possible combinations.

Example: =PERMUT(10, 4) returns 5,040.

RAND

RAND( )

The RAND function, which is always written without an argument in the parentheses, generates a decimal value with 15 digits to the right of the decimal point. You can then use that value in a formula.

Example: =IF((RAND()) > =.95, "Audit", "No audit").

RANDBETWEEN

    RANDBETWEEN(bottom, top)

The RANDBETWEEN function, which is new in Excel 2007, generates a random value between the values named in the *bottom* and *top* arguments, inclusive. The *bottom* value must be less than the *top* value.

Example: =RANDBETWEEN(1, 100)

TIP

RAND and RANDBETWEEN are volatile functions, which means that Excel regenerates the formula's result every time it recalculates your worksheet. If you want to fill a cell with a random number and not have that number change later, type a RAND or RANDBETWEEN formula in the formula bar, press F9, and then press Enter. Pressing F9 removes the formula from the cell but keeps the result.

ROUND

    ROUND(number, num_digits)

The ROUND function rounds *number* to the number of digits to the right of decimal point specified in the *num_digits* argument. The ROUND function rounds any digit of 5 or greater to the next higher value (e.g., it rounds 1.45 to 1.5 and 1.43 to 1.4). If the *num_digits* argument contains a negative number, the formula rounds the value that many places to the left of the decimal point.

Example 1: =ROUND(192.486, 2) returns the value 192.49.

Example 2: =ROUND(192.486, −1) returns the value 190.

ROUNDUP

> *ROUNDUP(number, num_digits)*

The ROUNDUP function rounds *number* to the number of digits to the right of the decimal point specified in the *num_digits* argument. Unlike the ROUND function, the ROUNDUP function always rounds a number up. If the *num_digits* argument contains a negative number, the formula rounds the value that many places to the left of the decimal point.

Example 1: =ROUNDUP(192.40001, 1) returns the value 192.5.

Example 2: =ROUNDUP(182.486, −1) returns the value 190.

ROUNDDOWN

> *ROUNDDOWN(number, num_digits)*

The ROUNDDOWN function rounds *number* to the number of digits to the right of the decimal point specified in the *num_digits* argument. Unlike the ROUND function, the ROUNDDOWN function always rounds a number down. If the *num_digits* argument contains a negative number, the formula rounds the value that many places to the left of the decimal point.

Example 1: =ROUNDDOWN(192.49999, 1) returns the value 192.4.

Example 2: =ROUNDDOWN(182.486, −1) returns the value 180.

SUBTOTAL

> *SUBTOTAL(function_num, ref)*

The SUBTOTAL summarizes the values in a range you specify using one of eleven functions. The advantage of using the SUBTOTAL function over, say, the SUM function, is that you can specify whether the SUBTOTAL function should include or exclude values that are hidden by a filter or that are contained in cells you hid by right-clicking a row or column head and then clicking Hide.

The table below lists the possible values for the *function_ num* arguments and the functions they represent. You can find detailed descriptions of the functions in the "Statistical Formulas" section at the end of this chapter.

Function_num (includes hidden values)	Function_num (excludes hidden values)	Function
1	101	AVERAGE
2	102	COUNT
3	103	COUNTA
4	104	MAX
5	105	MIN
6	106	PRODUCT
7	107	STDEV
8	108	STDEVP
9	109	SUM
10	110	VAR
11	111	VARP

Example 1: In the worksheet shown in Figure 3-1, the formula =SUBTOTAL(9, A2:A11) returns the value 55.

Example 2: In the worksheet shown in Figure 3-2, with rows 6 and 7 hidden, the formula =SUBTOTAL(109, A2:A11) returns the value 44.

NOTE

The formula in Example 1, =SUBTOTAL(9, A2:A10), includes hidden values in its calculation, so it would still return the value 55 if applied to the worksheet with hidden rows shown in Figure 3-2.

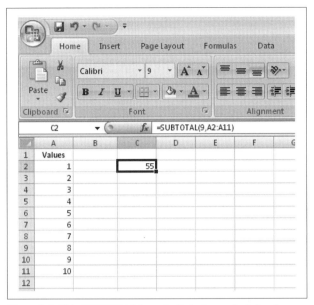

Figure 3-1. This SUBTOTAL formula finds the total of all values contained in the range A2:A11.

SUM

> *SUM(ref1, ref2…)*

The SUM function adds all of the values in the ranges specified in the *ref1*, *ref2*, and subsequent *ref* arguments.

Example: =SUM(A1, A5) adds the value in cells A1 and A5.

SUMIF

> *SUMIF(range, criteria, [sum_range])*

The SUMIF function finds the sum of cells in *range* that meet a given *criteria*. As an example, consider the data list shown in Figure 3-3.

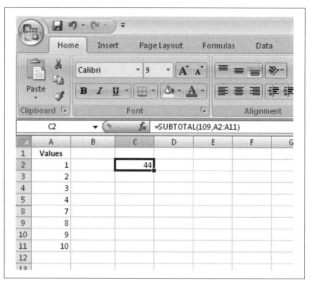

Figure 3-2. This SUBTOTAL formula limits its summary to the visible values in the range A2:A11.

The formula =SUMIF(A2:A11, ">=100") calculates the total of the cells in the range A2:A11 that contain values greater than or equal to 100.

You can also use the optional *sum_range* argument to have the SUMIF formula add values in a cell group other than that named in the *range* argument. In this case, the formula =SUMIF(A2:A10, ">=100", B2:B10) would add the values in column B that occur in the same rows as cells in A2:A10, which contain values that meet the *criteria*.

Example: Using the data found in Figure 3-3, the formula =SUMIF(A2:11, "<100") returns 306.

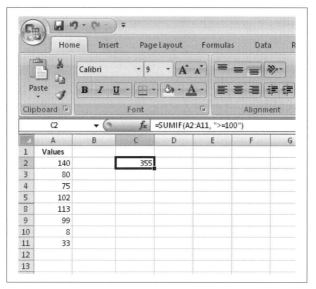

Figure 3-3. This SUMIF formula adds the values greater than or equal to 100 in the cell range A2:A11.

SUMIFS

> SUMIFS(sum_range, criteria_range1, criteria1, criteria_range2, criteria2...)

The SUMIFS function, which is new in Excel 2007, finds the sum of cells in *sum_range* that meet multiple criteria. As an example, consider the data list shown in Figure 3-4.

For this data set, the formula =SUMIFS(C2:C8, A2:A8, "=Monday", B2:B8, "=Lions") would add the values in column C that were found in rows where the value in column A is *Monday* and the value in column B is *Lions*.

Example: Using the data found in Figure 3-4, the formula =SUMIFS(C2:C8, A2:A8, "=Monday", B2:B10, ">=700") returns 1,397.

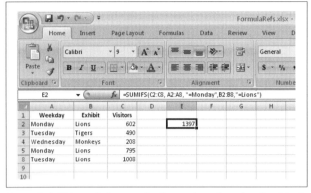

Figure 3-4. This worksheet tracks the number of people who visited a zoo's exhibits.

Date and Time Formulas

Excel represents dates and times using a number that indicates the number of days that have elapsed since January 1, 1900 (1/1/1900 is day 1). For example, January 15, 2008, is represented by the number 39462.

You use the digits to the right of the decimal point in a time/date number to indicate hours, minutes, and seconds. For example, the number 39462.5 indicates 12:00 PM.

Use the following functions to manipulate dates and times in your workbooks.

HOUR

> *HOUR(serial_number)*

> The HOUR function returns the hour component of a time, using the 24-hour clock (e.g., the hour for 1:00 PM is 13).

> Example: If cell A4 contains the time and date value 2/4/2008 7:14, the formula =HOUR(A4) would return 7.

MINUTE

> MINUTE(serial_number)

The MINUTE function returns the minute component of a time.

Example: If cell A4 contains the time and date value 2/4/ 2008 7:14, the formula =MINUTE(A4) would return 14.

MONTH

> MONTH(serial_number)

The MONTH function returns a number representing the month component of a date.

Example: If cell A4 contains the time and date value 2/4/ 2008 7:14, the formula =MONTH(A4) would return 2.

NOW

> =NOW()

The NOW() function returns the current date and time. Excel changes the function's result whenever it recalculates the worksheet that contains the formula.

SECOND

> SECOND(serial_number)

The SECOND function returns the second component of a time.

Example: If cell A4 contains the time 7:14:31, the formula =SECOND(A4) would return 31.

WEEKDAY

> WEEKDAY(serial_number, return_type)

The WEEKDAY function returns a number representing the weekday contained in a date and time *serial_number*. If the *return_type* argument is set to 1 or omitted, Sunday is day 1 and Saturday is day 7. If the *return_type* argument is set to 2, Monday is day 1 and Sunday is day 7. If the *return_type* argument is set to 3, Monday is day 0 and Sunday is day 6.

Examples: If cell A4 contains the date 2/4/2008, which is a Monday, the formula =WEEKDAY(A4) returns the value 2; the formula =WEEKDAY(A4, 2) returns the value 1.

YEAR

> *YEAR(serial_number)*

The YEAR function returns the year component of a date's *serial_number*.

Example: If cell A4 contains the date 2/4/2008, the formula =YEAR(A4) returns 2008.

Financial Formulas

Use the following functions to analyze financial data in your workbooks.

FV

> *FV(rate, nper, pmt, pv, type)*

The FV function calculates the future value of an investment into which you make periodic payments. The payments may not vary in amount or timing (that is, they must occur every month, quarter, or other period) and the interest rate must stay the same for the life of the investment.

Determining the correct value for the *rate* argument, which contains the investment's interest rate, can be a little tricky. The *rate* argument reflects the investment's interest rate divided by the number of payments made in a year. For example, if you made four payments per year into an investment with an 8% interest rate, the correct value for the *rate* argument would be 2%.

The *nper* argument contains the number of payment periods in the life of the investment. For example, if you made four payments per year for 15 years, the *nper* argument's value would be 60. The *pmt* argument contains the amount of the payment made into the investment every period, expressed as a negative number.

You can omit the *pmt* argument or set it to 0, but doing so means you must define a value for the *pv*, or present value, argument. Likewise, if you omit the *pv* argument or set it to 0, meaning that your investment has no monetary value until your first periodic payment, you must define a value for the *pmt* argument.

The final argument, *type*, indicates whether payments are due at the start or end of a payment period. The default value is 0, which indicates that payments are due at the end of the period. If you set the *type* argument to 1, Excel assumes the payments are made at the beginning of each period.

Example 1: For an investment returning 8% per year, with four payments of $1,000 per year for 15 years, the formula =FV(2%, 60, –1000) returns $114,051.54.

Example 2: For an investment returning 8% per year, with four payments of $1,000 per year for 15 years where the payments are made at the beginning of the payment cycle, the formula =FV(2%, 60, –1000, 1) returns $116,332.57.

IRR

 IRR(values, guess)

The IRR function calculates an investment's projected internal rate of return, or the effective interest rate received for a series of cash flows. Unlike the NPV (net present value) or FV (future value) function, the cash flows don't all have to be of the same value. The IRR function does require at least one negative value (usually representing the initial investment) and one positive value to calculate its result.

The *values* argument contains the projected cash flows; the optional *guess* argument contains your best guess as to the actual internal rate of return. If you omit the *guess* argument, which you usually will, Excel assumes a 10% starting point. If the program can't solve the IRR calculation within 20 attempts (the program uses an iterative process to approach the calculation's result), it displays a #NUM! error. If that happens, specify a value for the *guess* argument and press Enter to recalculate.

The following example uses the data values found in Figure 3-5.

Example: =IRR(C2:C6) returns 22%.

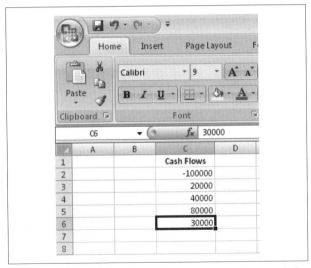

Figure 3-5. This worksheet lists an investment's cash flows, with the negative numbers representing payments into the investment.

NPV

> *NPV(rate, value1, value2…)*

In the NPV function, the *rate* argument specifies the investment's estimated rate of return, and the *value1* argument (and subsequent *value* arguments) are cell ranges that contain cash flows.

The NPV function calculates an investment's net present value based on a series of cash flows. The NPV function is related to the PV (present value) function, but the NPV function allows cash flows to occur at the start or end of a period. For example, the NPV formula lets you base your calculation on a $100,000 investment made today, or a $100,000 investment that's made over the next year.

All investments and losses (negative cash flows) must be expressed as negative numbers. Also, if the initial investment is made at the start of the project, you add the negative value to the NPV function's result so the calculation reflects that the money was spent as a sunk cost (that is, without the potential to earn income until after the entire investment was spent).

The following examples use the data values found in Figure 3-6.

Example 1: If the $500,000 investment occurs before the investment starts earning a return, you would use the formula =NPV(E2, C3:C5) + C2 to calculate the investment's net present value. The formula returns $163,215.27.

Example 2: If you made the $100,000 initial outlay over the first year of the investment, you would calculate the investment's net present value using the formula =NPV(E2, C2:C5), which returns $153.976.67.

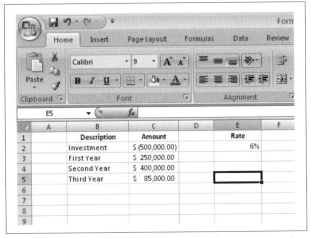

Figure 3-6. This data list contains the initial outlay and projected returns of an investment.

NOTE

An investment's internal rate of return is the interest rate at which the investment's net present value is 0.

PV

> *PV(rate, nper, pmt, fv, type)*

The PV function returns the present value of a series of an investment. For example, if you get a loan to buy a house, your lender could use the PV function to determine the value of your future payments if they wanted to sell the loan to another lender.

The *rate* argument specifies the investment's interest rate and *nper* specifies the number of payment periods. If you're making periodic payments into the investment, the *pmt* argument represents the amount of those payments. The amount must be the same and will be a negative number (indicating a cash outflow). You can set the *pmt* argument to 0 if you're making no payments into the investment.

The *fv* argument represents the future value of the investment (i.e., the target cash balance). If you set the *fv* argument to 0, you must specify a value for the *pmt* argument.

The *type* argument can be set to 0 (the default) or 1. If the *type* argument is set to 0 or is omitted, Excel assumes the payments occur at the end of each payment period. If it's set to 1, Excel assumes the payments occur at the start of each payment period.

Example: =PV(0.5%, 60, −1000), which represents the present value of a five-year loan (60 months) at 6% interest and a monthly payment of $1,000, returns a value of $51,725.56.

Lookup and Reference Formulas

Use the following functions to look up values from lists in your workbooks.

CHOOSE
> *CHOOSE(index_num, value1, value2…)*

The CHOOSE function lets you use cell inputs to select which of several values to use in a formula. The *index_num* argument specifies which value to look up; the *value1*, *value2*, and subsequent *value* arguments contain the values in the list. You can have up to 255 *value* arguments in a CHOOSE formula.

Example: =CHOOSE(2, 10%, 15%, 20%) returns 15%.

VLOOKUP
> *VLOOKUP(lookup_value, table_array, col_index_num, range_lookup)*

To visualize how the VLOOKUP function works, use the table of data shown in Figure 3-7 as a reference.

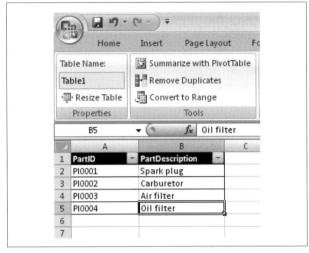

Figure 3-7. This Excel table contains the PartID values for inventory items at an auto supply shop.

The VLOOKUP function lets you look up a value in the first column of a table to find a value in another column, such as using the PartID of an automobile part to find the part's description. The VLOOKUP function's *lookup_value* argument contains either a value or the address of the cell that contains the value to be found in the table. The *table_array* argument contains the address of the table, the *col_index_num* argument is a number that indicates which column contains the values to be returned by the formula, and the *range_lookup* argument indicates whether the formula is required to find an exact match to return a result.

NOTE

You can use an Excel table's name as the value for the *table_array* argument, but you can't use a table column name in the *col_index_num* argument—you must use an integer value.

The *range_lookup* argument's default value is TRUE, which allows the function to find either an exact match for the *lookup_value* or to return the largest value that is smaller than the *lookup_value*. For example, if your list contained the dates July 1, July 2, and July 5, the *lookup_value* July 4 would return the entry for July 2. Setting the *range_lookup* argument to FALSE requires the function to find an exact match for the *lookup_value*.

IMPORTANT

If you set the *range_lookup* argument to TRUE, the table must be sorted in ascending order based on the values in the first table column.

The following examples use the simple table found in Figure 3-7.

Example 1: =VLOOKUP(N1, Table1, 2), with the value PI0001 in cell N1, returns Spark Plug.

Example 2: =VLOOKUP(N1, Table1, 2, FALSE), with the value PI0005 in cell N1, returns the #NA! error because the formula did not find an exact match.

HLOOKUP

> *HLOOKUP(lookup_value, table_array, row_index_num, range_lookup)*

The HLOOKUP function is very similar to the VLOOKUP function. The difference is that instead of using the VLOOKUP function to find values in vertical tables, where the values are arranged in columns, you use the HLOOKUP function to find values in horizontal tables, where the values are arranged in rows (such as in Figure 3-8).

The HLOOKUP function's *lookup_value* argument contains either a value or the address of the cell that contains the value to be found in the table's first row. The *table_array* argument contains the address of the table,

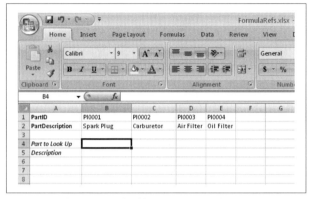

Figure 3-8. This horizontal table contains parts data, but in an unusual layout.

the *row_index_num* argument is a number that indicates which row contains the values to be returned by the formula, and the *range_lookup* argument indicates whether the formula is required to find an exact match to return a result.

The *range_lookup* argument's default value is TRUE, which allows the function to find either an exact match for the *lookup_value* or to return the largest value that is smaller than the *lookup_value*. For example, if your list contained the times 10:00 AM, 12:00 PM, and 2:00 PM, the *lookup_value* 1:30 PM would return the entry for 12:00 PM. Setting the *range_lookup* argument to FALSE requires the function to find an exact match for the *lookup_value*, which means that looking up 1:30 PM would return an error.

IMPORTANT

If you set the *range_lookup* argument to TRUE, the table must be sorted in ascending order based on the values in the first table row.

The following examples use the simple table found in Figure 3-8.

Example 1: =HLOOKUP(B4, A1:E2, 2), with the value PI0002 in cell B4, returns *Carburetor*.

Example 2: =HLOOKUP(B4, A1:E2, 2, FALSE), with the value PI0005 in cell B4, returns the #NA! error because the formula did not find an exact match.

Logical Formulas

Use the following functions to perform differing calculations when specified conditions are met.

IF

> IF(logical_test, value_if_true, value_if_false)

The IF function determines whether a cell's input meets a specified *logical_test*, such as whether an order is greater than $1,000. If the condition evaluates as TRUE, the function returns *value_if_true*; if FALSE, it returns *value_if_false*. As an example, consider the following formula:

> =IF(A5>100, "Free shipping", "Standard shipping")

TIP

Important: Any text you want the IF formula to display must be enclosed in double quotes.

Placing any value greater than 100 in cell A5 makes the formula return *Free shipping*; any value less than or equal to 100 makes the formula return *Standard shipping*.

The *value_if_true* and *value_if_false* arguments can also accept a formula. If you offered a 10% discount for all purchases over $100, the formula =IF(A5>100, A5/10, A5) would return the amount of the discount.

You can create a multilevel IF function, which tests for more than one condition, by placing an IF function in another IF function's *value_if_false* argument. Here's one example that allows free shipping for orders over $100 and $5 shipping for orders over $80 but less than $100:

=IF(A5>100, "Free shipping", IF(A5>80, "$5 shipping", "Standard shipping"))

NOTE

You can create IF formulas with up to 64 nested levels, but the VLOOKUP and HLOOKUP formulas are easier to create and maintain if you have more than three or four conditions to test.

Example: If cell A5 contains the value 75, the formula =IF(A5>100, 0, A5/10) returns 7.5.

IFERROR

  IFERROR(value, value_if_error)

The Excel team created the IFERROR function in response to customer requests to make it easier to display customized error messages. The *value* argument refers to a cell reference or calculation, such as *A11/A10*, that you want to test for an error. The *value_if_error* argument can contain a cell reference with the value to display or the text itself (which must be enclosed in double quotes).

Example: With the value 100 in cell A5 and the value 0 in cell A6, the formula =IFERROR(A5/16, "Error dividing the values!") displays the text *Error dividing the values!*

Text Formulas

Use the following formulas to manipulate text values in your workbooks.

CONCATENATE

    CONCATENATE(text1, text2, text3…)

The CONCATENATE function displays a series of text strings, contained in the formulas *text* arguments (*text1*, *text2*, etc.). The *text* arguments can contain either a cell reference or a text string enclosed in quotes.

Example: If cell A1 contains the value *books* and cell A2 contains the value *3*, the formula =CONCATENATE (A3, " ", A1) would return the string *3 books*.

LEFT

    LEFT(text, num_chars)

The LEFT function returns *num_chars* characters from the start of the text string named in the *text* argument.

Example: If cell A1 contains the value *PT301*, the formula =LEFT(A1, 3) returns the value *PT3*.

MID

    MID(text, start_num, num_chars)

The MID function returns characters from the middle of the text string specified in the *text* argument. The *start_num* argument indicates the first character to be returned, and the *num_chars* argument specifies how many characters to return.

Example: If cell A1 contains the text string *BR549ALT*, the formula =MID(A1, 3, 3) returns the string *549*.

RIGHT

    RIGHT(text, num_chars)

The RIGHT function returns *num_chars* characters from the end of the text string named in the *text* argument.

Example: If cell A1 contains the text string *BR549ALT*, the formula =RIGHT(A1, 3) returns the string *ALT*.

Statistical Formulas

Use the following functions to summarize your worksheet data using statistical techniques.

AVERAGE
>   *AVERAGE(number1, number2…)*

The AVERAGE function finds the numeric average of the values in the ranges named in the *number* arguments. Each *number* argument can be a number or a cell reference.

Example: If cells A1:A3 contain the values 7, 8, and 9, then =AVERAGE(A1:A3) returns 8.

AVERAGEIF
>   *AVERAGEIF(range, criteria, [average_range])*

The AVERAGEIF function calculates the average of values that meet a given criteria. As an example, consider the data list shown in Figure 3-9.

The formula =AVERAGEIF(C2:C6, ">=500") calculates the average of the cells in the range C2:C6 that contain values greater than or equal to 500.

You can also use the optional *average_range* argument to have the AVERAGEIF formula average values in a cell group other than that named in the *range* argument. In this case, the formula =AVERAGEIF(A2:A6, "=Lions", B2:B16) would average the values in column B that occur in the same rows as cells in A2:A16 which contain values that meet the criteria.

Example: =AVERAGEIF(B2:B6, "=Lions", C2:C6) returns 801.6667.

AVERAGEIFS
>   *AVERAGEIFS(average_range, criteria_range1, criteria1, criteria_range2, criteria2…)*

The AVERAGEIFS function, which is new in Excel 2007, finds the average of cells in a list that meet multiple

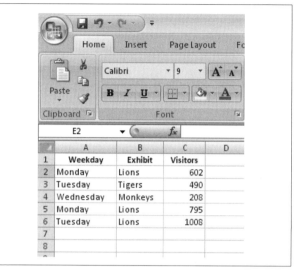

Figure 3-9. You can use the AVERAGEIF function to discover how many visitors you get on high-volume days.

criteria. As an example, consider the data list shown in Figure 3-10.

For this data set, the formula =AVERAGEIFS(C2:C6, A2:A6, "=Monday", C2:C6, ">=1000") would average the values in column C that were found in rows where the value in column A is Monday and the values in column C are greater than or equal to 1000.

Example: =AVERAGEIFS(C2:C6, A2:A6, "=Monday", C2:C6, ">=1000") returns 1404.

COUNT

> *COUNT(value1, value2…)*

The COUNT function counts the number of cells in a range that contain numbers, dates, or textual representations of numbers. The *value* arguments contain cell references or values to be examined.

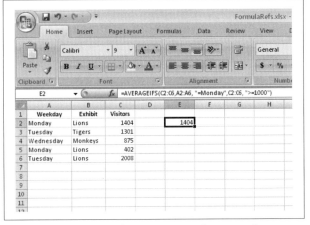

Figure 3-10. You can use the AVERAGEIFS function to discover how many visitors you average at specific exhibits on high-volume days.

Example: If cells A1:A3 contain a number, cell A4 contains a date, and cell A5 contains the word FALSE, the formula =COUNT(A1:A5) returns 4.

COUNTA

    COUNTA(value1, value2…)

The COUNTA function counts the number of non-empty cells in a range. The *value* arguments contain cell references or values to be examined.

Example: If cells A1:A3 contain dates, cell A4 is blank, and cells A5:A6 contain names, the formula =COUNTA(A1:A6) returns 5.

COUNTBLANK

    COUNTBLANK(range)

The COUNTBLANK function counts the number of empty cells in *range*.

Example: If cells A1:A3 contain dates, cell A4 is blank, and cells A5:A6 contain names, the formula =COUNT-BLANK(A1:A6) returns 1.

COUNTIF

> COUNTIF(range, criteria)

The COUNTIF function counts the number of cells in *range* that meet a given *criteria*. As an example, consider the worksheet shown in Figure 3-11.

Using this worksheet, the formula =COUNTIF(B2:B11, "=Spark Plugs") would return 4.

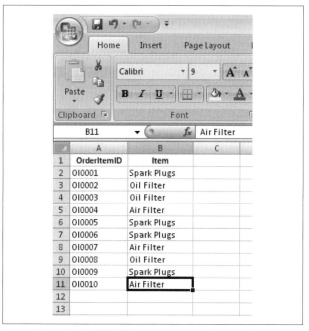

Figure 3-11. The COUNTIF function lets you determine how many times a particular value, or set of values, occur within a data list.

You can use the question mark (?) and asterisk (*) wildcards to create more flexible *criteria*. The question mark matches any single character, while the asterisk matches any number of characters. For example, the criteria "=C*" matches the name *Curt*; the criteria "=C?", which looks for exactly one character after the letter "C", does not.

If you want to count cells that contain an asterisk or question mark, type a tilde in front of the character (e.g., "=~?" or "=Ctrl-~*").

Example 1: =COUNTIF(B2:B11, "=Oil Filter") returns 3.

Example 2: =COUNTIF(B2:B11, "=*Filter") returns 6 (the count of all items that end with the characters *Filter*).

COUNTIFS

> COUNTIFS(range1, criteria1, range2, criteria2...)

The COUNTIFS function counts the number of cells in a range that meet multiple criteria. The *range* arguments contain cell ranges, while the *criteria* arguments contain rules the function uses to test the worksheet's values. As with the COUNTIF function, you must enclose the COUNTIFS function's *criteria* within double quotes.

The following examples use the worksheet shown in Figure 3-12.

Example 1: =COUNTIFS(B2:B11, "=Oil Filter", C2:C11, "=Local")

Example 2: =COUNTIFS(B2:B11, "=*Filter", C2:C11, "=In-store")

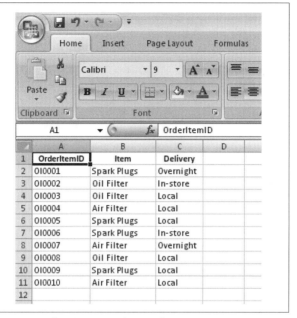

Figure 3-12. The COUNTIFS function lets you count occurrences within a data list based on values in multiple columns.

FORECAST

> FORECAST(x, known_y's, known_x's)

The FORECAST function uses linear regression to predict a value based on existing data. One such data series appears in Figure 3-13.

The *known_y's* argument represents the dependent array of values. In this case, those values are a product's sales figures. The *known_x's* argument contains the independent array of values, the year. The *x* argument contains a cell reference or value for which you want to predict a future value given the existing data.

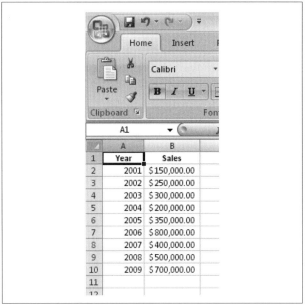

Figure 3-13. The FORECAST function estimates future results based on past performance.

Example: Using the data shown in Figure 3-13, the formula =FORECAST(E2, B2:B10, A2:A10) returns the value $718,055.56 with the year 2010 input into cell E2.

MAX

> MAX(number1, number2...)

The MAX function returns the largest value described by the *number* arguments. The *number* arguments may contain numbers or references to cell ranges that contain numbers.

Example: =MAX(1, 5, 3, 7, 2) returns 7.

MEDIAN

> *MEDIAN(number1, number2…)*

The MEDIAN function finds the middle value of a set of *number* values. If there are an even number of values in the set, the MEDIAN function returns the average of the two values in the middle of the set.

Example 1: =MEDIAN(1, 3, 5, 7, 8, 9, 11) returns 7.

Example 2: =MEDIAN(1, 3, 5, 7, 8, 9, 11, 14) returns 7.5.

MIN

> *MIN(number1, number2…)*

The MIN function returns the smallest value described by the *number* arguments. The *number* arguments may contain numbers or references to cell ranges that contain numbers.

Example: =MIN(5, 3, 7, 2) returns 2.

MODE

> *MODE(number1, number2…)*

The MODE function returns the value that occurs most frequently in the data set described by the *number* arguments. The *number* arguments may contain numbers or references to cell ranges that contain numbers.

NOTE

If two values occur equally frequently, the MODE function returns the value it encounters first in the data set.

Example: =MODE(1, 2, 3, 2, 3, 4, 5, 2) returns the value 2.

PRODUCT

> *PRODUCT(number1, number2…)*

The PRODUCT function multiplies the values described by the *number* arguments. The *number* arguments may contain numbers or references to cell ranges that contain numbers.

Example: =PRODUCT(1, 8, 9, .5) returns 36.

STDEV

> *STDEV(number1, number2...)*

The STDEV function calculates the standard deviation of the values in a range using a sample of the values in the range. The *number* arguments may contain numbers or references to cell ranges that contain numbers.

Example: =STDEV(1, 9, 14, 20, 17, 3, 27) returns the value 9.327379053.

NOTE

The STDEV function might return slightly different results based on the sample values Excel chooses to use in the calculation.

STDEVP

> *STDEVP(number1, number2...)*

The STDEVP function calculates the standard deviation of the values in a range using all values in the range (the "P" at the end of the function name indicates that the function uses the entire population of the data set in its calculation). The *number* arguments may contain numbers or references to cell ranges that contain numbers.

Example: =STDEVP(4, 14, 9, 18, 27, 3) returns the value 8.341662504.

VAR

> *VAR(number1, number2...)*

The VAR function calculates the variance of the values in a range using a sample of the values in the range. The *number* arguments may contain numbers or references to cell ranges that contain numbers.

Example: =VAR(1, 9, 14, 20, 17, 3, 27) returns the value 87.

NOTE

The VAR function might return slightly different results based on the sample values Excel chooses to use in the calculation.

VARP

The VARP function calculates the variance of the values in a range using all values in the range (the "P" at the end of the function name indicates that the function uses the entire population of the data set in its calculation). The *number* arguments may contain numbers or references to cell ranges that contain numbers.

Example: =VARP(4, 14, 9, 18, 27, 3) returns the value 69.58333333.

CHAPTER 4

Excel Reference

This chapter provides reference information that is hidden within Excel, including:

- Useful Excel commands that are not on any toolbar or menu by default (Table 4-1)
- Native data and graphic file formats (Tables 4-2 and 4-3)
- Startup switches to control how Excel launches (Table 4-4)
- Wildcard characters used in Excel searches and filters (Table 4-5)
- Default locations of important files and folders (Table 4-6)

This chapter also lists default keyboard shortcuts for the following types of tasks:

- General program and navigational shortcuts (Tables 4-7 and 4-8)
- Data entry and formatting (Tables 4-9 through 4-13)
- Manipulating shortcut menus (Table 4-14)
- Creating and manipulating charts (Table 4-15)
- Working with macros (Table 4-16)
- Displaying and hiding items in a PivotTable (Table 4-17)
- Using Smart Tags (Table 4-18)

Command Reference

There are hundreds of commands available in Excel 2007; there wasn't room for them all on the Ribbon. Table 4-1 lists some of the useful commands that you can find in the "Commands Not in the Ribbon" list in the Excel Options dialog box's Customize page. (To display that list, click Office Button → Excel Options → Customize. Click the "Choose commands from" down arrow, and click "Commands Not in the Ribbon".) You can use the techniques in Chapter 2 to make these commands available. You can find any others in Help.

Table 4-1. Useful Excel commands

Command	Action	Suggested uses
Publish As Web Page	Displays the Publish dialog box accessed from the Save As Web Page dialog box.	Add button to the Quick Access Toolbar to facilitate publishing worksheets to the Web.
Web Page Preview	Displays the worksheet as if it were a web page.	Add button to the Quick Access Toolbar to facilitate publishing worksheets to the Web.
Select Visible Cells	Selects only the visible cells (those not hidden by a filter).	Add button to the Quick Access Toolbar to avoid selecting hidden cells.
Constrain Numeric	Requires users to enter numbers into the selected cells.	Add to the Quick Access Toolbar when setting data validation rules.
Cycle Font Color	Change cell text to the next color in the Font Color palette.	Add to the Quick Access Toolbar.
Scenario	Displays a list of scenarios available for the active worksheet.	Add list box to the Quick Access Toolbar for use in presentations.
Lighting	Changes the lighting sources and characteristics for objects on a worksheet.	Add button to the Quick Access Toolbar when you edit drawing objects.
Calculator	Displays the Windows calculator for quick calculations.	Add button to the Quick Access Toolbar for calculations that don't involve data in the worksheet.

Table 4-1. Useful Excel commands (continued)

Command	Action	Suggested uses
Close All	Closes all open workbooks but does not exit Excel.	Add button to the Quick Access Toolbar if you work with lots of workbooks at a time.
New	Creates a new workbook without displaying the New Workbook dialog box.	Add button to the Quick Access Toolbar to create new workbooks quickly.

Native Formats

Excel 2007 supports many common structured data and graphic formats without the need to filter the files. Table 4-2 lists all of the structured data formats Excel understands without the need for conversion, and Table 4-3 displays the native graphics formats. If you can't find a filter for the file format you want to use in Excel, look on the Office web site, the Office installation disk, and the program manufacturer's web site to see if a filter is available.

Table 4-2. Native file formats

Format	File extension
Microsoft Excel 2007 Workbook	.xlsx
Microsoft Excel 2007 Macro-enabled Workbook	.xlsm
Microsoft Excel 2007 Template	.xltx
Microsoft Excel 2007 Macro-enabled Template	.xltm
Microsoft Excel 2007 Binary Workbook	.xlb
Microsoft Excel 97–2003 Workbook	.xls
Microsoft Excel 5.0/95 Workbook	.xls
Microsoft Excel 97–2000 & 5.0/95 Workbook	.xls
Microsoft Excel 4.0/3.0/2.1 Worksheet	.xls
Microsoft Excel 4.0 Workbook	.xlw
Microsoft Excel 97–2003 Template	.xlt
XML Data	.xml

Table 4-2. Native file formats (continued)

Format	File extension
XML Spreadsheet	.xml
Web Page	.mht
Web Archive	.htm
Text Files	.txt
Comma Separated Values	.csv
Data Interchange Format	.dif
Symbolic Link Format	.slk

Table 4-3. Native image file formats

Format	File extension
Graphics Interchange Format	.gif
Joint Photographic Experts Group	.jpg .jpeg
Portable Network Graphics	.png
Windows bitmap	.bmp
Tagged Image File Format	.tiff
Windows Enhanced Metafile	.emf
Windows Metafile	.wmf
Vector Markup Language	.vml
Microsoft Windows Media	.avi, .asf, .asx, .rmi, .wma, .wax, .wav

Startup Switches

As with most programs, you can start Excel from the command line (Start → Programs → Accessories → Command Prompt). At the command prompt, type **excel.exe** to run Excel just as you would if you ran the program by selecting it from the Programs menu. When you run Excel from the command prompt, however, you have the option of adding startup switches that change how the program opens.

Table 4-4 lists the startup switches available to you for Excel (e.g., excel.exe /e).

Table 4-4. Startup switches

Startup switch	Description
`workbook path/file name`	Open a specific workbook.
`/r workbook path/file name`	Open a specific workbook as a read-only file.
`/e`	Prevent display of the Excel startup screen and a new blank workbook.
`/p folder path/folder name`	Specify the working folder.
`/s`	Start Excel in Office Safe Mode, which runs the main program with no add-ins or templates.
`/a progID`	Starts Excel and loads the named add-in.
`/t workbook path/file name`	Starts Excel and loads the named file as a template.

Wildcards in Filters and Searches

When you need to find particular kinds of values in your worksheets, you can use the "Find and Replace" dialog box (opened to the Find tab page by clicking Home → Find & Select → Find, or to the Replace tab page by clicking Home → Find & Select → Replace) or filters. Excel extends your search power by letting you use wildcards, which are characters that can take on multiple values (for example, any letter or any character). Table 4-5 lists the wildcard characters you can use in Excel searches and filters.

Table 4-5. Excel wildcard characters

Character	Description
?	Any single character (e.g., "fr?e" finds "frye" and "free").
*	Any group of characters (e.g., "f*" finds "frye", "fair", and "foul").
~ followed by ?, *, or ~ finds a question mark, asterisk, or tilde	"Frye~?" finds "Frye?".

Default File Locations

Table 4-6 lists the locations of important files and folders for Excel 2007. You can change some of the locations; others you can't. (You may have configured your Documents folder differently or installed Office in an unusual location. This table lists the defaults.)

Table 4-6. Default file locations

File or location	Operating system	Path	User-definable
Document Storage	Windows Vista	C:\Documents and Settings\ <username>\Documents	Yes
	Windows XP	C:\Documents and Settings\ <username>\My Documents	Yes
User Templates	Windows XP and Vista	C:\Documents and Settings\ <username>\Application Data\Microsoft\Templates	Yes
AutoRecover Files	Windows XP and Vista	C:\Documents and Settings\ <username>\Application Data\Microsoft\Excel	Yes
Startup directory	Windows XP and Vista	C:\Documents and Settings\ <username>\Application Data\Microsoft\Excel\ XLSTART	Yes
Program Files	Windows XP and Vista	C:\Program Files\Microsoft Office\Office12	No
History of recently opened documents	Windows XP and Vista	C:\Documents and Settings\ <username>\Application Data\Microsoft\Office\ Recent	No

Keyboard Shortcuts

Excel has literally hundreds of predefined key combinations that let users who prefer to use the keyboard perform a wide variety of tasks. The most common shortcuts—Ctrl-S to save a workbook, and Ctrl-P to print—are there, as are many others.

The following tables are grouped to make finding shortcuts easier. Each group concentrates on a related set of activities, such as navigating a workbook, entering data, or selecting and editing data.

NOTE

If you define custom keyboard shortcuts using any of the listed combinations, your custom shortcut will override the default shortcut.

Table 4-7. General program shortcuts

Key	Action
Ctrl-N	Create a new workbook.
Ctrl-O or Ctrl-F12	Open a workbook.
Ctrl-S or Shift-F12	Save a workbook (the Save As dialog box appears if this is the first time you're saving the workbook).
F12	Open the Save As dialog box to specify the name and location of the workbook.
Ctrl-W or Alt-F4	Close the active workbook. If it is the only open workbook, close Excel as well.
F1	Open Help, display the Microsoft Excel Help task pane, or open the Office Assistant.
F7	Run the Spelling checker.
F10	Display keyboard shortcuts for the visible Ribbon commands.
Shift-F10	Open a shortcut menu.
Ctrl-F9	Minimize the workbook.
Ctrl-F10	Restore or maximize the workbook.
Ctrl-P or Ctrl-Shift-F12	Open the Print dialog box.
Alt-Tab	Switch to the next program.
Alt-Shift-Tab	Switch to the previous program.
Ctrl-Esc	Open the Windows Start menu.
Prtscn	Copy a picture of the screen to the clipboard.
Alt-Prtscn	Copy a picture of the active window to the clipboard.

Table 4-8. Navigate a worksheet

Key	Action
Up arrow	Move the active cell up one row.
Down arrow	Move the active cell down one row.
Left arrow	Move the active cell left one column.
Right arrow	Move the active cell right one column.
Home	Move to the beginning of the current row.
Ctrl-Home	Move to the beginning of the worksheet (usually cell A1).
Ctrl-End	Move the last cell in the worksheet (at the intersection of the last used row and last used column).
Page Up	Scroll up one screen.
Page Down	Scroll down one screen.
Alt-Page Up	Scroll right one screen.
Alt-Page Down	Scroll left one screen.
Ctrl-Page Up	Move to the previous worksheet in the workbook.
Ctrl-Page Down	Move to the next worksheet in the workbook.
Shift-F11	Insert a new worksheet.
Ctrl-Shift-Page Down	Select the current and next sheet.
Ctrl-Shift-Page Up	Select the current and previous sheet.
Ctrl-F6	Go to the next open workbook.
Ctrl-Shift-F6	Go to the previously viewed open workbook.
F6	Move between the split panes of a workbook.
Shift-F6	Move back to the previously viewed pane of a split workbook.
Ctrl-G	Open the GoTo dialog box.
Ctrl-F	Open the Find page of the "Find and Replace" dialog box.
Ctrl-H	Open the Replace page of the "Find and Replace" dialog box.
Ctrl-Alt-Right arrow	Move clockwise between nonadjacent selections.
Ctrl-Alt-Left arrow	Move counterclockwise between nonadjacent selections.

Table 4-9. Selecting data and cells

Key	Action
Ctrl-C	Copy a cell's contents or the selection on the formula bar.
Ctrl-X	Cut a cell's contents or the selection on the formula bar.
Ctrl-V	Paste the contents of the clipboard into the cell or onto the formula bar.
Ctrl-Space	Select the entire column.
Shift-Space	Select the entire row.
Ctrl-A	Select the entire worksheet.
Shift-Backspace	With multiple cells selected, select only the active cell.
Ctrl-Shift-Space	With an object selected, select all objects on a sheet. With a cell selected, select all cells.
Ctrl-6	Alternate between hiding objects, displaying objects, and displaying placeholders for objects.
Ctrl-Shift-8 or Ctrl-*	Select the current region around the active cell (the data area enclosed by blank rows and blank columns). In a PivotTable report, select the entire PivotTable report.
Ctrl-Shift-0	Select all cells that contain comments.
Ctrl-\	In a selected row, select all cells with different values than the active cell.
Ctrl-Shift-|	In a selected column, select all cells with different values than the active cell.
Ctrl-[	Select all cells that contain a value that affects the value of any cell in the selection.
Ctrl-Shift-{	Select all cells that contain a value that directly or indirectly affects any cell in the selection.
Ctrl-]	Select all cells that contain a formula that directly references the active selection.
Ctrl-Shift-}	Select all cells that contain formulas that directly or indirectly reference the active cell.
Alt-;	Select the visible cells in the current selection.
Shift-Right arrow	Expand the selection one cell to the right.
Shift-Left arrow	Expand the selection one cell to the left.
Shift-Up arrow	Expand the selection up one cell.
Shift-Down arrow	Expand the selection down one cell.

Table 4-9. Selecting data and cells (continued)

Key	Action
Ctrl-Shift-Right arrow	Expand the selection right to the last nonblank cell on the row.
Ctrl-Shift-Left arrow	Expand the selection left to the last nonblank cell on the row.
Ctrl-Shift-Up arrow	Expand the selection up to the last nonblank cell in the column.
Ctrl-Shift-Down arrow	Expand the selection down to the last nonblank cell in the column.
Shift-Home	Expand the selection to the beginning of the row.
Ctrl-Shift-Home	Expand the selection to the beginning of the worksheet.
Ctrl-Shift-End	Expand the selection to the end of the worksheet.
Shift-Page Down	Extend the selection down one screen.
Shift-Page Up	Extend the selection up one screen.
Ctrl-F1	Show or hide the Ribbon toolbar.
Shift-F8	Add another range of cells to the selection.

Table 4-10. Data entry

Key	Action
Enter	Add data to a cell and move to the cell below the active cell.
Alt-Enter	Insert a line break in the active cell.
Ctrl-Enter	Fill selected cells with the value in the active cell if the formula bar is active.
Shift-Enter	Add data to a cell and move to the cell above the active cell.
Tab	Add data to a cell and move to the cell to the right of the active cell.
Shift-Tab	Add data to a cell and move to the cell to the left of the active cell.
Esc	Cancel cell entry.
Arrow keys	When a cell is selected, move to an adjacent cell. When editing within a cell, move one character in the direction of the arrow.
Home	Move to the beginning of the line.

Table 4-10. Data entry (continued)

Key	Action
F4 or Ctrl-Y	Repeat the last action.
Ctrl-D	Fill from the active cell down to the last cell in a selection.
Ctrl-R	Fill from the active cell to the right-most cell in a selection.
Ctrl-K	Insert a hyperlink.
Ctrl-;	Insert the date.
Ctrl-Shift-:	Insert the time.
Ctrl-Z	Undo the last action.

Table 4-11. Working with formulas

Key	Action
=	Begin entering a formula.
Enter	Complete cell entry and move to the cell below the active cell.
Esc	Cancel cell entry.
Shift-F3	When entering a formula, display the Insert Function dialog box.
Ctrl-A	When the insertion point is to the right of a function name, display the Function Arguments dialog box for that function.
Ctrl-Shift-A	When the insertion point is to the right of a function name, insert the argument names and parentheses into the formula.
F3	Paste the name of a named range into the formula.
Alt-=	Insert a SUM formula into the cell.
F9	Recalculate all formulas in all open workbooks.

Table 4-12. Edit data

Key	Action
F2	Position the insertion point after the last character in the selected cell.
Backspace	Clear the contents of the active cell, or delete one character to the left of the insertion point.

Table 4-12. Edit data (continued)

Key	Action
Delete	Delete the character to the right of the insertion point, or delete the contents of the active cell.
Ctrl-Delete	Delete text to the end of the line.
F7	Open the Spelling dialog box.
Shift-F2	Edit a cell comment.

Table 4-13. Format data

Key	Action
Alt-'	Open the Style dialog box.
Ctrl-1	Open the Format Cells dialog box.
Ctrl-Shift-~	Format the cell's contents with the General number format.
Ctrl-Shift-$	Format the cell's contents with the Currency number format.
Ctrl-Shift-%	Format the cell's contents with the Percentage number format.
Ctrl-Shift-#	Apply the Date format as day, month, and year.
Ctrl-Shift-@	Apply the Time format with hour, minutes, and AM or PM.
Ctrl-Shift-!	Apply the Number format with two decimal places, thousands separator, and minus sign for negative values.
Ctrl-B	Apply or remove bold formatting.
Ctrl-I	Apply or remove italics.
Ctrl-U	Apply or remove underlining.
Ctrl-5	Apply or remove strikethrough.
Ctrl-9	Hide selected rows.
Ctrl-Shift-(	Unhide hidden rows within the selection.
Ctrl-0	Hide selected columns.
Ctrl-Shift-)	Unhide hidden columns within the selection.
Ctrl-Shift-&	Add an outline border to the selected cells.
Ctrl-Shift-_	Remove all borders from the selected cells.

Table 4-14. Manipulating shortcut menus

Key	Action
Shift-F10	Display the shortcut menu for the selected item.
Alt-Space	Display the Excel control menu.
Down arrow	When a menu is open, select the next command.
Up arrow	When a menu is open, select the previous command.
Left arrow	Select the menu to the left; in a submenu, switch between the main menu and submenu.
Right arrow	Select the menu to the right; in a submenu, switch between the main menu and submenu.
Home	Select the first command on the open menu.
End	Select the last command on the open menu.
Esc	Close the open menu. In a submenu, close the submenu but keep the menu open.

Table 4-15. Create and manipulate charts

Key	Action
F11 or Alt-F1	Create a chart using the data in the current range.
Ctrl-Page Down	Select the next sheet in the workbook.
Ctrl-Page Up	Select the previous sheet in the workbook.
Down Arrow	Select the previous group of elements in a chart.
Up Arrow	Select the next group of elements in a chart.
Right Arrow	Select the next element in a group.
Left Arrow	Select the previous element in a group.

Table 4-16. Work with macros

Key	Action
Alt-F8	Open the Macro dialog box.
Alt-F11	Open the Visual Basic Editor.
Ctrl-F11	Insert a Microsoft Excel 4.0 macro sheet.

Table 4-17. Display and hide items in a PivotTable

Key	Action
Up arrow	Select the previous item in the range.
Down arrow	Select the next item in the range.
Right arrow	For an item that has lower-level items available, display the lower-level items.
Left arrow	For an item that has lower-level items displayed, hide the lower-level items.
Home	Select the first visible item in the list.
End	Select the last visible item in the list.
Enter	Close the list and display the selected items.
Space	Check, double-check, or clear a checkbox in a list. Double-check selects both an item and all of its lower-level items.
Tab	Switch among the list, the OK button, and the Cancel button.

Table 4-18. Smart Tags

Key	Action
Alt-Shift-F10	Display the menu or message for a Smart Tag. If more than one Smart Tag is present, move to the next Smart Tag and display its menu or message.
Down arrow	Select the next item in a Smart Tag menu.
Up arrow	Select the previous item in a Smart Tag menu.
Enter	Perform the action for the selected item in the Smart Tag menu.
Esc	Close the Smart Tag menu or message without taking action.

CHAPTER 5

Excel Resources

Internet Sites

Microsoft's Official Excel Site
Official news and articles plus tips and tricks.

http://www.microsoft.com/office/excel

Office Update
Microsoft's update site for Office, which includes security patches, program updates, and new add-ons.

http://office.microsoft.com/ProductUpdates/default.aspx

Microsoft TechNet
A knowledge base of technical articles and reference materials on the gamut of Microsoft products.

http://www.microsoft.com/technet

Woody's Watch
Woody Leonhard's advice, news, and newsletters on Microsoft Office applications, including Excel.

http://www.woodyswatch.com

Office Zealot
A collection of blogs on topics relating to Microsoft Office.

http://www.office-zealot.com

John Walkenbach's Spreadsheet Page
A collection of how-to articles and solutions on advanced Excel topics.

http://j-walk.com/ss

Excel Most Valued Professional (MVP) Site
> David McRitchie hosts an Excel section on the Microsoft MVP site. You can find answers to advanced questions and other MVP sites.
>
> *http://www.mvps.org/dmcritchie/excel/excel.htm*

Excel Newsgroups
> Microsoft runs a news server that hosts a number of Excel-related newsgroups. You can read the newsgroups using Outlook Express or Internet Explorer 5.0 or later.
>
> The news server is *news://msnews.microsoft.com*; the Excel newsgroups all start with *microsoft.public.excel*.

Microsoft Template Gallery
> Microsoft offers templates for all of the Office programs, including Excel.
>
> *http://search.officeupdate.microsoft.com/ TemplateGallery*

Books

Microsoft Office Excel 2007 Step by Step, Curtis Frye, Microsoft Press
> A self-paced training book that enables you to learn how to use Excel 2007 at your own speed.

Excel 2007: The Missing Manual, Matthew MacDonald, O'Reilly
> A comprehensive reference for Excel 2007.

Excel Hacks, Second Edition, David Hawley and Raina Hawley, O'Reilly
> A set of techniques you can employ to make Excel 2007 even more useful.

Excel 2007 Formulas, John Walkenbach, Wiley
> A comprehensive guide to creating Excel formulas, with detailed examples of many functions.

Microsoft Office Excel 2007 Visual Basic for Applications Step by Step, Reed Jacobson, Microsoft Press

A self-paced training book that enables you to build your Excel 2007 programming skills.

Programming Excel with VBA & .NET, Jeff Webb and Steve Saunders, O'Reilly

A comprehensive guide to learning how to write professional-quality code in Excel.

Excel Utilities

Power Utility Pak v7

A useful collection of add-ins that add new functionality to Excel 2007. The text-handling routines and ability to force Excel 2007 to recognize imported values as numbers (which it sometimes has trouble with) are worth the price of admission. Also available for previous versions of Excel.

http://j-walk.com/ss/pup/pup7/index.htm

Ribbon Customizer

An Excel 2007 add-in that gives you much, but not complete, control over the Excel 2007 Ribbon interface. The Ribbon Customizer generates the RibbonX code required to create your own command groups, customize individual commands, remove existing tabs, and so on. Free Starter Edition and 30-day trial of the Professional Edition.

http://pschmid.net/office2007/ribboncustomizer/index.php

Crystal Xcelsius from Business Objects

A powerful program that enables you to create interactive Excel charts and dashboards, which you can integrate into PowerPoint, Word, PDF, and web files. Free trial available.

http://www.xcelsius.com

XLStat

XLStat is a collection of Excel data analysis utilities from Addinsoft that can mine your Excel data for information about customers, sales processes, and more. The range of advanced analytical tools is impressive—a godsend if you don't have the time to write the functions yourself. Free trial available.

http://www.xlstat.com/indexus.html

ASAP Utilities

A collection of free utilities you can download that perform useful Excel tasks, such as coloring a specific row or copying a worksheet's page and print settings.

http://www.asap-utilities.com

DigDB Excel Add-in Toolkit

This utility package includes routines that let you fill a selected area with random data, create queries you could normally only perform in Access, fix broken links, and sort data based on multiple criteria. Free trial available.

http://www.digdb.com

eTools for Excel

From BaRaN Systems, a collection of add-ins ranging from quality control management to generating calendars. Quite useful to have around the office.

http://www.baran-systems.com

Business Spreadsheets

A collection of templates that help with business forecasting, multiple regression analysis and forecasting, portfolio optimizing, and developing investment hedging strategies. Most templates have a 30-day trial, while others are free.

http://www.business-spreadsheets.com

Index

We'd like to hear your suggestions for improving our indexes. Send email to *index@oreilly.com*.